The Microwave Master

DONOVAN ▾JON▾FANDRE

IN ASSOCIATION WITH
IRV HAMILTON

▾ ▾ ▾

KQED, Inc.

Managing Editor:
Linda Brandt

Designer:
Salinda Tyson

Photographer:
Nikolay Zurek

Food Stylist:
Joanne Dexter

Photo Assistant:
Stephen Siegelman

Printing Coordinator:
Interprint

Props for Photography:
Macys by Appointment
Forrest Jones Inc.

Library of Congress Catalogue Card Number: 88-80681

ISBN 0-912333-01-4

▼

This book is dedicated to all
the people who are
committed to using
their microwave ovens for
more than just reheating
leftovers.

TABLE OF CONTENTS

▼ ▼ ▼

▼ ▼ ▼

A Word About
Microwave Cooking

"If you're a good cook, using a microwave oven will make you an even better cook. If you're a lousy cook, your microwave oven will only make you a faster, lousy cook."

A number of years ago, when I first began cooking with a microwave oven, I relied on trial and error to learn how to use it best and convert my favorite recipes for microwave cooking. At that time, people couldn't imagine how it was possible to cook anything worth eating in one of those new machines. And they very often told me so.

But over the years, through classes, demonstrations, books, media appearances and my own television shows—such as "The Microwave Master" on public television—I've had an opportunity to tell literally millions of people about microwave cooking.

Today microwave cooking is accepted as a very useful and time-efficient method of preparing food. I certainly haven't been the only one telling the microwave story. But I'm pleased to be part of what really is an on-going revolution in the way we cook.

People are using their microwave ovens more and more. However, a lot of microwave oven owners still don't realize how many different ways they can put this wonderful cooking appliance to use.

In this book, I want to help you expand your microwave cooking repertoire. But, the intent isn't just to give you new recipes. Just as I did years ago, I want to encourage you to experiment and to adapt your favorite conventional recipes for microwave cooking.

Sure, it still involves a little trial and error. But doing so will make your microwave oven an even

Now that you know something about it, use it. As with anything in your kitchen, that's the only way you'll master it and let it begin working for you.

People have been frying, baking, broiling and sautéeing things in their kitchens for centuries. But microwave technology is new, so it's no wonder that people are unfamiliar with, and maybe a little uneasy about, using microwaves to prepare food.

more valuable tool in your kitchen. And trying new things is one of the things that makes cooking so much fun.

Microwave Cooking

There are three kinds of cooking.

Convection is cooking with the use of heated air. It's what makes your traditional oven work. "Convection" ovens, which have recently become popular, are simply more efficient versions of your old oven.

Conduction is where the heat is transferred by contact with a hot surface. It's how a skillet or frying pan cooks.

Cooking by radiation uses energy that radiates from a source and is transferred to the food without coming in contact with another medium. This is what happens when you broil a steak over charcoal or make toast in a toaster.

It's also the way microwave energy cooks. But there's a big difference between your grill and your microwave oven. Unlike a grill, the microwave energy doesn't radiate heat. Instead, the energy causes water molecules within the item being cooked to vibrate. That creates the heat which cooks the food.

Quick and Easy Microwave Cooking

There's a long list of benefits to microwave cooking.

1. The oven remains cool, and so does your kitchen. This is a real benefit in warm weather. It also means you can open the oven at any time to check the progress of a dish and not lose heat as you would with a conventional oven.

2. Cooking times are greatly reduced. In most cases, you can complete the cooking in anywhere from a half to a quarter of the conventional cooking time. Often you'll save even more time. But there are cases where your microwave oven will not do the job any faster. Cooking pasta is an example. You can do it just as quickly on the stovetop.

More important than just cooking faster, microwave ovens cook things beautifully. If microwave
ovens cooked things faster, but not as well as conventional cooking, they would have been a fad that came
and quickly disappeared.

3. Cut back on your fat intake. Nutritionists keep
telling us we eat too much animal fat. But we've
grown accustomed to the taste of butter or other fats
in our diet because we use so much of it in the
cooking process.

With microwave cooking, you can cut off virtually
all visible fat from meat before cooking and it won't
dry out. You can also eliminate fats used to prevent
dishes from sticking to the pan.

**4. By cooking and serving in the same dish, there's
less dishwashing to do.** Microwave cookware has
been designed to be attractive as well as functional.
Many dishes are available in decorator colors to match
your serving decor.

Tips from Donovan

If you've been using your microwave oven for real
cooking, you probably already know how to use it
well. But if you're one of the many people who
haven't quite mastered the art here are some tips
I think are particularly important.

1. Read the manual. Take a little time to read the
manual that comes with your microwave oven. That
way you'll be able to make best use of its features.
Your oven will probably do things you didn't even
know about when you bought it.

2. Undercook everything. If a recipe calls for 5
minutes of cooking, set the timer for 4 minutes, 30
seconds and check on how it's coming along. It's easy
to add a little cooking time to make it just right. But
there's not much you can do about a dish that's
overcooked.

And remember, the cooking process will continue
for a bit after the microwave oven has been turned off,

just as with other forms of cooking. When you're cooking to a particular temperature, stop about 10 degrees short of what you want the final temperature to be. The residual cooking will finish the job.

3. Covering food during cooking can be important. Some types of recipes—steamed and poached dishes, for example—require covered cooking to retain the moisture and prevent drying. Much of the microwave cookware available today is equipped with lids for this purpose. For lidless dishes, use plastic wrap.

4. Plan your cooking. Dense items such as carrots and potatoes take longer to cook than do less dense ingredients. Due to their density, they also retain heat longer. So if you're preparing, say, potatoes and a fish filet, cook the potatoes first. Set them aside and then cook the fish, which only takes a short time. The potatoes will remain heated.

5. Use your microwave oven for those things it does best. Think of your microwave oven as just another tool for cooking. It's capable of doing many things well, but not everything. Use it for casseroles, steaming, sauteeing, poaching, roasting, reheating and thawing.

Unless a recipe calls for something to be crusted, seared or dried, your microwave oven is probably the best way to cook it. But broiled lamb chops belong on a grill. And an angel food cake can best be done in a conventional oven.

6. Don't be afraid of making a mistake. Experiment and try new things. So what if something doesn't turn out just the way you want it to? Next time do it a little differently. I still keep a big dog around to dispose of my mistakes.

When you get right down to it, cooking is cooking is cooking. All you're really doing is preparing, seasoning and heating food. The microwave oven is just another way of doing it. The recipes in this book have been developed specifically for use with a microwave oven. That doesn't mean you can't use your microwave oven to prepare dishes you learned from your mother.

Ovens and Accessories

Microwave cooking has come a long way since the first time I gave it a try. Ovens are far more sophisticated and a wide variety of cookware and accessories is now available. In fact, it's actually gotten confusing because of all the choices. So remember these points when you go shopping.

1. Microwave Ovens: Only buy the oven features you need or want. Ovens today run the gamut from the simple, compact versions to ones that are literally equipped with computers.

Pick the one that meets your needs and has the features you want. Remember that you'll probably end up using it a lot more than you think. So, as with buying a car, carefully evaluate the features before you make a decision.

Be sure you get an oven that has adequate power for your requirements, variable power settings and is simple to use.

2. Essential Accessories: Invest in a few important accessories. If you've seen me on television or doing a demonstration, you know I always keep an instant-reading thermometer in my pocket. This is a very useful tool. You poke it into the dish you're cooking, check the temperature and then cook it more if it needs it. It takes the guesswork out of all cooking, whether microwave or conventional.

Microwave cookware manufacturers have taken the traditional ring mold and made a microwave version of it. I suggest every microwave cook buy one because it's perfect for dishes that require a large quantity of ingredients. The cone in the center allows microwave energy to penetrate more effectively during the cooking process.

Roasting racks are another useful piece of microwave cookware. Made of plastic or ceramic, they have ridges on which the item being cooked rests which allow the juices and fat to drain off. That reduces the amount of retained fat in the food.

You don't think of aluminum as being a useful microwave cooking accessory, but it is. Read the

A woman in one of my classes told me how her husband had complained that her cooking just didn't taste as good after they got a microwave oven. One day she prepared an elegant meal in her microwave oven, and just before he arrived, she put the dishes in her conventional oven. After sampling the fare, he proceeded to compliment her on how much better everything tasted since she'd gone back to her old oven.

manual that comes with your oven and learn how to use metal for shielding during cooking. By covering the legs and wings of a chicken or turkey during part of the cooking you'll prevent them from becoming overcooked and dried out.

The list of things you can buy for microwave cooking goes on and on. Just be sure to remind your friends and relatives that you have a microwave oven a few weeks before your birthday and the holidays.

Just one final note. I truly appreciate the letters and cards so many of you have sent to me. Your comments and observations have been very helpful in determining the content of my programs and even this book.

They also reaffirm the fact that people are becoming more and more comfortable with microwave cooking and increasingly creative in the ways in which they're using it.

Appetizers

▼

Easy Eggplant Spread

*Mushroom Spread
(Duxelles)*

Mushroom-Nut Spread

Mint Omelet

*Crab Timbales with
Cheese Sauce*

Spinach Timbales

*Omelet-Stuffed
Peppers with
Tomato Sauce*

Party Paté

Potstickers

Italian Meatballs

Frozen Vegetable Ring

*Bread Bowl with
Spicy Cheese Dip*

*Cheese-Shrimp Fondue
with Dilled Bread Cubes*

*Pickled Shrimp with
Spicy Dipping Sauce*

Caviar-topped Potatoes

▼ ▼ ▼

▼ ▼ ▼

A microwave oven is a wonderful tool for preparing and reheating many kinds of hors d'oeuvres and appetizers. As you'll see, I've included a wide choice of spreads, dips, pates, steamed dishes and poached delicacies all cooked by microwave.

But it won't do all of the popular snack dishes. Missing are those delicious fried or pastry-covered items that require hot fat or hot air to prepare them properly.

I love those fatty, salty things. But you just can't make them taste as good in a microwave oven as you can by conventional means. So prepare appetizers both ways. Use your microwave oven for the ones it does best. And fry or bake the recipes most suited to that form of cooking.

▼ ▼ ▼   Easy Eggplant Spread

1 large eggplant, cut into
1-inch cubes

1 onion, chopped or 1
package (12 oz.) frozen
chopped onions

1 green pepper, chopped
or 1 package (10 oz.)
frozen chopped peppers

4 tablespoons fresh
garlic, minced

1 can (10 oz.) stewed
tomatoes

1 tablespoons fresh
ground pepper

2 tablespoons lemon
juice

I love to serve this at parties. It's a healthy spread, low in fat, rich in fiber and delicious. But it can also be used with toast at breakfast or as a topping for baked potatoes.

1. Place all ingredients, except lemon juice, in a 3-quart casserole. Cover and cook at 100% power (high) for 30 minutes. Stir and cook at 100% power (high) 15 minutes longer. Mash together, or process slightly. Add lemon juice.
2. You might think 45 minutes is a long time to cook a dish in a microwave oven. This is necessary to cook off the water and achieve the proper consistency.

▼ ▼ ▼   Mushroom Spread (Duxelles)

1 pound fresh
mushrooms, sliced

1 medium onion, finely
chopped

2 tablespoon butter or
margarine

This simple spread really shows off the delicate and complex flavors of these wonderful edible fungi. Cooking by microwave provides a great way to reduce the water content of mushrooms without lengthy conventional cooking.

Wrap sliced mushrooms in paper towels. Cook at 100% power (high) 5 minutes. Press out excess water.

1. Place mushrooms in 2-quart casserole. Add onion and butter . Cook at 100% power (high) 4 minutes or until very soft.
2. Place in blender and process until smooth. Serve hot or cold on toast or crackers.

▼ ▼ ▼

Mushroom-Nut Spread

1 cup unsalted nuts (such as peanuts or almonds)
1 medium onion, chopped
3 pounds mushrooms, thickly sliced
3 tablespoons sesame seeds

Together, the nuts and mushrooms make this spread rich, creamy and truly delicious.

1. Place nuts and onion in 3-quart casserole. Cook at 100% power (high), covered, for 3 to 4 minutes or until the onions are soft.
2. Wrap mushrooms in a kitchen towel and cook at 100% (high) for 5 minutes. Allow to cool.
3. Twist the towel to extract as much moisture as possible. Add to nut and onion blend. Add seeds and process in a blender until smooth. If watery, cook the finished butter at 100% (high) for a couple minutes, checking to avoid overcooking.

▼ ▼ ▼

Mint Omelet

TO SERVE 4

12 large mint leaves, chopped
½ cup chopped Italian parsley
6 large eggs
2 tablespoons bread crumbs
⅔ cup grated pecorino or Parmesan cheese

As Carlo Middione told me on one of my shows, "This is another use, in addition to juleps, for all that mint in your yard." I know you'll enjoy this fragrant and delicately flavored frittata.

1. Mix mint leaves, Italian parsley, eggs, bread crumbs and cheese thoroughly. Pour into a buttered 1-quart, oval dish.
2. Cook at 100% (high), uncovered, 4 to 5 minutes, stirring twice. Allow to stand for 2 minutes. Loosen sides and invert onto a serving platter. Cut into slices and serve.

Original recipe appears in Carlo Middione's *The Food of Southern Italy*, published by William Morrow and Company, Inc., 1988.

▼ ▼ ▼ Crab Timbales with Cheese Sauce

TO SERVE 6

1 pound crab meat or imitation crab meat
½ pint heavy cream
4 eggs
1 teaspoon dried dill weed
¼ teaspoon cayenne pepper
½ cup Parmesan cheese

The French word "timbale" means kettledrum. In French cuisine, timbales are small dishes of custard made in molds that resemble drums. I enjoy using crab for these delicate appetizers. If real crab isn't available, imitation crab will work just fine.

1. Chop crab into small pieces.
2. Mix with cream, eggs, dill weed, cayenne pepper and Parmesan cheese. Pour into cups of microwave muffin pan.
3. Cover with plastic wrap and cook at 100% (high) 6 to 7 minutes, or until set.
4. Remove from muffin pan by placing a plate over the top and inverting.

▼ ▼ ▼ Spinach Timbales

TO SERVE 6

1 pound tofu, firm
2 egg whites
1 cup imitation bacon bits
1 package (10 oz.) frozen chopped spinach, thawed and squeezed of water
2 tablespoons butter or oil
½ cup Parmesan cheese

Some people tell me they don't like tofu because it's too bland. That's the beauty of it. It's an excellent source of protein that you can flavor any way you like. Made from soy beans, it completely cholesterol free.

1. Mix tofu, egg whites, bacon bits, spinach, butter or oil, Parmesan cheese and MicroShake together. Pour into muffin pan or 6 custard cups. Place custard cups in microwave oven separated by at least 1 inch. Cook at 100% power (high) 4 to 6 minutes, or until set.
2. Serve with picante sauce or fresh tomato sauce (see page 19).

▼ ▼ ▼

Omelet-stuffed Peppers with Tomato Sauce

TO SERVE 4

Fresh Tomato Sauce

2 large tomatoes, peeled and cut up

1 medium onion, chopped

2 garlic cloves, chopped

2 tablespoon olive oil

1 tablespoon dried Italian herbs

Stuffed Peppers

4 yellow, red, or green bell peppers

1 medium onion, chopped

½ pound Italian sausage or 1 cup chopped ham

6 large eggs, beaten

1 cup shredded cheese, such as cheddar, Swiss or Colby

Prepared salsa for garnish (optional)

If you're looking for a unique way to prepare an omelet for a special brunch or party, this is ideal. Try this version. Then use your imagination and make up your own combinations.

1. Place tomatoes, onion, garlic, olive oil and Italian herbs in cook-and-measure bowl. Cook at 100% power (high), uncovered, for 10 minutes, stirring once.

2. Cut off top of peppers. Discard stems and set tops aside. Remove seeds and membrane. Place peppers upright in 3-quart casserole or ring pan. Cover and cook at 100% power (high) for 4 minutes.

3. Chop tops of peppers and combine with sausage and onion. Cover and cook at 100% power (high) for 3 to 4 minutes. Discard fat.

4. Combine meat mixture with eggs and cheese. Spoon into whole peppers. Cover and cook at 70% (medium-high) for 3 to 4 minutes, or until eggs set. Note: If you're watching cholesteral, substitute artificial eggs for the real ones or use only the egg whites.

5. Top with tomato sauce or prepared salsa.

▾ ▾ ▾

Party Paté

TO SERVE 6 TO 10

1 medium onion, chopped

2 tablespoon butter

2 packages (10 oz.) frozen chopped spinach, thawed and squeezed of water

1 pound ground beef

½ pound ground turkey or veal

1 pound bulk pork sausage

1 cup bread crumbs

2 tablespoon dried Italian herbs

2 tablespoon fresh parsley, chopped

¼ cup capers or green peppercorns

1 egg

Pates and meat loaves are easy to make by microwave. The main reason is the container doesn't get hot so you don't have to protect the food from burning. In fact, any time you see a recipe that calls for a water bath or bain-marie (in which one pan cooks inside another containing water), you can make it easier and in considerably less time in your microwave.

1. In a 1½-quart cook-and-measure bowl, cook onion and butter at 100% power (high) for 3 to 4 minutes.

2. Mix with spinach, ground beef, turkey or veal, pork sausage, bread crumbs, Italian herbs, parsley, capers or green peppercorns and egg. Place in 2-quart ring pan. Cover with wax paper or a plate. Cook 70% power (medium-high) for about 15 minutes, or to a temperature of 160 degrees.

3. Drain off fat and juices. Allow to cool slightly and press down to increase density. Drain juices again. Invert onto a serving platter.

Potstickers

▼ ▼ ▼

TO SERVE 7

Filling

- 5 dried black mushrooms, soaked and chopped
- ½ pound lean ground pork
- 2 green onions, minced
- 1¼ cups Chinese cabbage, finely chopped
- 2 tablespoons sesame oil
- 1 teaspoon minced fresh ginger
- ½ teaspoon sugar
- 28 won ton wrappers
- ½ cup cooking oil
- 2 tablespoons water

Dipping Sauce

- ½ cup soy sauce
- ¼ cup rice vinegar
- 1 tablespoon chilli oil

Potstickers have become a very popular item in Chinese restaurants and my friend Martin Yan does them beautifully. I showed him how well they worked in a microwave browning skillet.

1. Mix together mushrooms, pork, green onions, Chinese cabbage, sesame oil, ginger and sugar. Place about 1 tablespoon of filling on each won ton wrapper. Raise the edges of the dough and bring them together like the foil covering of a chocolate kiss. Crimp the dough with your fingers to close it.

2. Preheat browning skillet in microwave oven following instructions on skillet package. Dip bottom of each pot sticker in oil and place as many as will fit on browning skillet.

3. Add tablespoons water and cover with a metal pie pan. Cook at 100% power (high) for 3 to 4 minutes, or until bottom of potstickers turn brown and crisp and the top is properly steamed. The metal pie pan will reflect the microwave energy away from the top of the potstickers and avoid drying them as they cook.

4. Repeat until all pot stickers are done. Place sauce in bowl on center of table so everyone can dip.

Original recipe appears in Martin Yan's *The Chinese Chef*, published by Doubleday and Company, Inc., 1985.

▼ ▼ ▼ # Italian Meatballs

1 pound lean ground beef

¼ pound bulk Italian sausage, hot

1 cup Italian-style bread crumbs

1 tablespoon dried Italian herbs

¼ teaspoon dried red pepper flakes

1 egg

¼ cup dry red wine

Salt and pepper

MicroShake (optional)

These tasty meatballs can be used in spaghetti sauce or as an hors d"oeuvre. If you want them less spicy (Remember the "spicy meatball" commercial?), use sweet Italian sausage and leave out the pepper flakes.

1. Mix ground beef, sausage, bread crumbs, Italian herbs, red pepper flakes, egg, red wine, salt, pepper and MicroShake together and form into 1-inch balls.

2. Place around the outer edge of a 3-quart casserole fitted with a steamer insert. Cover and cook at 100% power (high) for 4 minutes.

3. Stir to relocate balls for even cooking. Recover, and cook at 100% power (high) for 3 additional minutes, or until meatballs reach 160 degrees.

4. Add to your favorite spaghetti sauce and heat through.

▼ ▼ ▼ # Frozen Vegetable Ring

1 package (16 oz.) frozen peas and carrots

1 package (16 oz.) frozen corn

1 package (16 oz.) broccoli cuts

6 eggs

1½ cups buttermilk

½ cup low-sodium Parmesan cheese

2 tablespoon dried Italian herbs

One of the most useful pieces of microwave cook- ware you can have in your kitchen is the ring mold. It allows the microwave energy to penetrate the ingredients evenly and the ring-shaped finished product makes for a very attractive presentation.

1. Place the peas and carrots, corn and broccoli in alternating layers in a 3-quart ring mold. Cover securely with plastic wrap and cook at 100% (high) for 12 to 15 minutes.

2. Press down on the top of the cooked vegetables to compact them, and drain off the liquid.

3. Mix together eggs, buttermilk, cheese and herbs. Pour over vegetables and mix thoroughly. Cook at 100% (high), uncovered, for 12 to 15 minutes or until the custard has set.

4. Allow to cool and unmold onto a platter. Slice and serve.

▾ ▾ ▾

Bread Bowl with Spicy Cheese Dip

TO SERVE 4

1 large round loaf of
sourdough bread
(1½ lb.)

1 pound process cheese

1 can (14.5 oz.) Mexican-
style tomatoes and
chilis

1 green pepper, chopped
or 1 package (6 oz.)
frozen, chopped green
peppers

1 can (10.5 oz.) condensed
cheddar cheese soup

Bread sticks and/or
chips

Celery and carrot sticks

Broccoli and
cauliflower flowerets,
raw

Any round, high loaf of bread, such as French or
Italian, will do for this dish. But San Francisco
sourdough is the best. If you don't live in California,
impose on a traveling friend to bring back a loaf for
you.

1. Cut a 5-inch diameter circle off the top of the
   bread crust. Remove bread from inside of the
   loaf, leaving about 1 inch of crust and bread all
   around. Save the bread for use as stuffing or
   bread crumbs.
2. Cook the remaining loaf at 100% power (high)
   about 5 minutes, uncovered, to harden.
3. Cook cheese, tomatoes and chilies, peppers and
   soup at 100% power (high) in a 1½-quart cook-
   and-measure bowl, covered, on high for 6 to 8
   minutes, or until cheese is soft and ingredients
   blended. Stir to combine and pour into bread
   shell.
4. Dip with bread cubes, raw vegetables, chips or
   bread sticks. When the dipping is done, break
   apart the crust and enjoy.

▼ ▼ ▼

Cheese-Shrimp Fondue with Dilled Bread Cubes

TO SERVE 4

Dilled Bread Cubes

6 thick slices of buttered
  French bread
  Dried dill weed

Fondue

1 cup dry white wine

2 cups Swiss cheese,
  shredded (natural, not
  processed)

2 tablespoons cornstarch

1 pound fresh cooked
  shrimp or 1 package
  (10 oz.) frozen cooked
  shrimp, defrosted

1 tablespoons dried dill
  weed

This was the most popular cheese dish at my Fondue Pot restaurant in Marin County, just north of San Francisco. Here's a version you can make easily at home. In addition to serving it in the traditional way with bread cubes, it makes a superb cheese sauce for vegetables.

1. Sprinkle bread with dill and place under broiler to lightly brown. Remove. Cut in cubes and set aside.

2. Place wine in 1½-quart cook-and-measure bowl. Cook at 100% power (high) high 2 to 3 minutes or until wine starts to boil.

3. Coat cheese with cornstarch and dill weed. Add ½ of cheese to wine and stir. Cook at 100% (high), uncovered, for 1 minute, stirring once.

4. Add remainder of cheese and cook at 100% (high), uncovered, 1 minute more. Stir until smooth.

5. Add shrimp and stir. Transfer to chafing dish or fondue pot and serve with dilled bread cubes

▼ ▼ ▼

Pickled Shrimp with Spicy Dipping Sauce

TO SERVE 4

1 pound large shrimp (16-21 count), peeled and deveined

½ cup white cider vinegar

2 tablespoon pickling spice

1 tablespoon Dijon mustard

1 tablespoon horseradish or wasabi

3 tablespoon minced chives

1 teaspoon cornstarch

The piquant flavor of pickling spices enhance the taste of shrimp. I serve this dish as a sidedish or an hors d'oeuvre.

1. Place shrimp, vinegar, pickling spice, mustard, horseradish and chives in 1-quart casserole.
2. Cover and cook at 100% (high) 4 to 6 minutes or until shrimp are firm and cooked.
3. Drain juices and place in small covered bowl or dish. Cover shrimp and chill both shrimp and juices overnight in refrigerator.
4. To make the dipping sauce, add cornstarch to the juices, stir and cook at 100% (high) until thick, about 2 to 3 minutes.
5. Cool sauce and dip shrimp to coat before serving.

▼ ▼ ▼

Caviar-topped Potatoes

TO SERVE 4

¾ pound new potatoes, well scrubbed

½ pint sour cream

1 small jar caviar (choose red or imported black varieties, or domestic varieties such as golden)

Here's a simple-to-make, festive appetizer that will impress any guest. Just hollow out the center of cooked new potatoes, fill with a little sour cream or herb-flavored cheese spread, and top with a tiny amount of caviar.

1. Place new potatoes in a 3-quart casserole dish. Cook, covered, at 100% power (high) for 6 to 8 minutes or until tender but still firm.
2. When cool, slice off a thin piece from the bottom of each potato so that it will stand upright.
3. Scoop out centers of each potato with small spoon or melon baller. Fill with sour cream or cheese spread and top with a small amount of caviar.
4. (A simple variation: Fill steamed snow peas with the sour cream or cheese spread and offer alongside.)

Soup

▼

*Chilled Vegetable
Gazpacho*

Easy Vegetable Soup

Hasty Vegetable Soup

Corn Chowder

French Onion Soup

Potato-Onion Soup

Cabbage Stoup

Clam Chowder

Dilled Carrot Soup

Cheddar Cheese Soup

▼ ▼ ▼

▼ ▼ ▼

Generally, when a recipe calls for a lot of water, the microwave oven is not the most efficient tool to use. Boiling water on the range top takes much less energy than in your microwave oven.

Why then, do we encourage you to make soup in your microwave oven? The main reason is your microwave oven turns off automatically after the cooking time has elapsed. That means you can be cooking soup while you're away from the kitchen; working or playing.

Simply put the ingredients in a pot, set the timer and take off. You don't have to worry about the soup boiling away.

If you want a super-fast soup, cook the ingredients in your microwave oven and the stock on the range. Combine the two and you have a perfect soup in a fraction of the time it would take using conventional cooking.

Chilled Vegetable Gazpacho

TO SERVE 4

1 package (10 oz.) frozen broccoli

1 package (10 oz.) frozen green beans

2 medium onions

1 green pepper, cored and sliced

2 cups peeled and chopped cucumber

2 cups chopped tomato

2 cups bloody mary mix

1 can (14 1/2 oz.) stewed tomatoes

Chopped chives for garnish

Not everything I prepare is done in a microwave oven. So for a change of pace—particularly on a warm, sunny day—here's how I make this refeshshing, South American chilled soup.

1. In a blender or food processor, process the broccoli, beans, onions and peppers until they are coarsely chopped.
2. Add cucumber, tomatoes and bloody mary mix to other vegetables. Mix thoroughly and process.
3. Serve topped with chopped chives (fresh or frozen) and/or a dollop of plain yogurt.

Easy Vegetable Soup

TO SERVE 4

1 package (16 oz.) frozen mixed vegetables

1 quart homemade chicken stock or 1 can (32 oz.) chicken broth

1 tablespoon Italian herbs

When you think of soup you imaging a pot simmering all afternoon on the stove. That's not so with this double-quick soup using microwave and traditionally cooking.

1. Place vegetables in a 3-quart casserole dish, cover and cook at 100% power (high) for 8 to 10 minutes.
2. In the meantime, bring stock or broth to a boil in a large pan on the stove. Add herbs and simmer for 2 minutes. Note: Homemade stock has much less sodium than canned broth.
3. Add broth to cooked vegetables, mix and serve.

▼ ▼ ▼   # Hasty Vegetable Soup

TO SERVE 6–8

7 ounces pepperoni
   sausage, chopped

1 pound hot or sweet
   Italian sausage

½ package (7 oz.) frozen
   chopped peppers

½ package (4 oz.) frozen
   chopped onions

1 package (10 oz.)
   frozen Italian-style
   beans

2 tablespoons dried
   Italian herbs

1 can (15 oz.) garbonzo
   beans or other bean
   of your choice

1 can (28 oz.) crushed
   tomatoes

3½ cups chicken broth
   Grated Parmesan
   cheese

When time is short and you want a hearty soup you can prepare in minutes, this is the answer. For a more elegant dish, it can be pureed and served with a dollop of sour cream or plain yogurt.

1. In 3-quart casserole, cook at 100% power (high), covered, pepperoni and sausage for 6 to 7 minutes. Drain off fat and crumble Italian sausage.

2. Add peppers, onions and beans. Cover and cook at 100% power (high) for 10 minutes, stirring once. Add Garbonzo beans.

3. In the meantime, on your stovetop, heat almost to boiling the tomatoes and chicken broth. Add them to the contents of the 3-quart casserole.

4. Serve topped with Parmesan cheese.

▾ ▾ ▾   # Corn Chowder

TO SERVE 4

4 slices bacon

1 medium yellow onion,
   chopped

1 package (10 oz.) frozen
   whole-kernel corn

2 tablespoon flour

12 ounces milk

   Freshly ground pepper

I'm a big fan of chowders, those rich and thick soups.
Corn makes some of the best I've ever tasted.

1. Place bacon on microwave broiling rack or on a
    plate. Cover with paper towel to prevent
    spattering. Cook at 100% power (high) for about
    4½ minutes. Check for doneness and cook for
    15 to 20 second more, if needed. Let cool and
    crumble.

2. Place onion in 3-quart casserole dish, and cook,
    uncovered, at 100% power (high) for 3 minutes,
    or until the onion is soft.

3. Add corn and stir to mix. Cook, covered, at 100%
    power (high) for 5 minutes.

4. Add flour, whisking to mix. Cook at 100% power
    (high), covered, for 1 to 2 minutes.

5. Add milk and pepper. Stir to mix. Cook at 100%
    power (high), covered, for 5 minutes. Note: For
    a richer chowder, use cream or half-and-half
    instead of milk.

6. Top with crumbled bacon when serving.

▼ ▼ ▼

French Onion Soup

TO SERVE 4

5 large yellow onions,
  thinly sliced
½ cup butter or
  margarine
4 cups beef broth
1 cup croutons
8 ounces grated Swiss
  cheese
  Grated Parmesan
  cheese

While traditional French chefs may grimace at the
idea of making onion soup in a microwave oven, I
found it to be simple. It tastes great and even has the
gooey cheese on top.

1. Put onions and butter or margarine in 3-quart
   casserole dish. Cover and cook at 100% power
   (high) for 8 to 10 minutes, or until onions are
   soft.
2. Heat broth to boiling on the stove.
3. Divide onions into 4 microwaveable soup bowls.
   Fill with broth, top with croutons or rusks and
   Swiss cheese. Sprinkle Parmesan cheese on top.
4. Return to microwave and cook at 100% power
   (high) for 4 to 6 minutes, or until Swiss cheese
   melts.

▾ ▾ ▾

Potato-Onion Soup

TO SERVE 4

4 medium yellow onions, chopped

5 medium red potatoes, peeled (or unpeeled) and sliced

4 tablespoons sweet butter

1 cup chicken stock or canned chicken broth

3 cups milk

Salt and freshly ground pepper

Chopped chives for garnish

Potato-leek soup is well-known and very elegant. I've substituted yellow onions because they're less expensive and have a wonderful flavor. But, if you like, use leeks.

1. Place onions, potatoes and butter in a 3-quart casserole dish. Cook, covered, at 100% power (high) for 20 minutes, or until potatoes are cooked. In a food processor or blender, puree and set aside.

2. In the meantime, simmer stock in a pot on the stove top. Add milk, stir and continue to heat to nearly boiling.

3. Add pureed vegetables and season with salt and pepper.

4. Garnish each serving with chives.

▾ ▾ ▾

Cabbage Stoup

TO SERVE 6

1 medium onion, chopped

2 medium potatoes, unpeeled and diced

1 rutabega, diced (optional)

1 small cabbage, chopped

1 pound Polish or smoked sausage, sliced

4 cups chicken broth

Freshly ground pepper

Because this dish is a little like a stew and a little like a soup, I call it a "stoup." It's a hearty, simple and inexpensive whole meal.

1. Place onion, potatoes and rutabega in 3-quart casserole. Cover and cook at 100% power (high) 10 to 12 minutes or until potatoes are tender.

2. Stir in cabbage and sausage. Cover and cook at 100% power (high) for 8 to 10 minutes. Season with pepper to taste.

3. Add heated broth, stir and serve.

▼ ▼ ▼

Clam Chowder

TO SERVE 4

1 large Russet potato, diced

1 medium onion, chopped

2 slices bacon, chopped

2 tablespoon butter

2 tablespoon flour

2 cups chopped steamed clams or 2 cans (6.5 oz.) chopped clams

1 cup clam juice

1 cup condensed milk

1 cup milk

Freshly ground pepper

Hot sauce to taste (optional)

There are hundreds of versions of this New England classic. This is my personal favorite.

1. Place potatoes, onions and bacon in 2-quart ring pan. Cover and cook at 100% power (high) for 8 to 10 minutes, or until potatoes are tender.
2. Add butter and flour. Stir until blended.
3. Add clams, juice and milk. Cover and cook at 100% power (high) for about 10 minutes or until broth starts to thicken. Season with pepper and hot sauce.

▾ ▾ ▾   # Dilled Carrot Soup

TO SERVE 6

6 large carrots, peeled
  and coarsely chopped

2 medium onions,
  coarsely chopped

2 stalks celery, sliced

3 cups chicken broth

½ teaspoon salt

¼ teaspoon white pepper

¼ teaspoon dried
  dill weed

  Green onions, for
  garnish

  Sour cream, for
  garnish

Ordinary vegetables become thick, full-flavored soups using this simple method. First cook the vegetable in the microwave with a few seasonings and then whirl the ingredients together in a food processor or blender until smooth. This recipe combines carrots, onions, celery, chicken broth, and dill weed. But try other seasonal vegetables such as squash, potatoes, broccoli or cauliflower. Serve soup warm or at room temperature, or chilled.

1. Place carrots, onions, 1 cup of the chicken broth, salt, and pepper in a 3-quart casserole dish.
2. Cook, covered, at 100% power; (high) for 4 to 5 minutes or until vegetables are soft.
3. Transfer to a food processor or blender. Process until smooth. With motor running, add remaining 2 cups broth until blended.
4. Ladle soup into individual bowls and garnish each with a few thin slices of green onion and a dollop of sour cream.
5. (For a thicker soup, substitute one cup half-and-half for one of the cups of chicken broth added in Step 3.)

▼ ▼ ▼

Cheddar Cheese Soup

TO SERVE 6

1 cup chopped onion
1 cup chopped celery
1 cup chopped carrot
4 tablespoons butter
¼ cup flour
¼ cup water
2 tablespoons prepared
  mustard
2 tablespoons
  Worcestershire sauce
1 cup milk
1 quart homemade
  chicken stock or
  canned chicken broth
½ pound shredded
  cheddar cheese
¼ cup chopped parsley

Cheese soups are rich and creamy. Cheddar is especially well suited for soup making, but don't hesitate to experiment with other cheeses you enjoy.

1. Put onion, celery, carrots, butter, flour, mustard, Worcestershire sauce and water in 3-quart casserole dish. Cook, covered, at 100% power (high) for 5 minutes or until the vegetables are soft.

2. In the meantime, heat milk and broth in a pot and heat on the stove top. When hot, add cheese and simmer until cheese has melted.

3. Add cheese mixture to vegetables. Cook at 100% power (high), uncovered, for 2 to 3 minutes to thicken the soup.

4. Garnish with chopped parsley.

▼

Salad,
Rice
&
Pasta

▼

Hot Shrimp Salad

Red Potato Salad

Potato Salad

*Egg Salad with
Watercress*

*Warm Lamb Salad
with Peanut &
Black Currant Dressing*

Pasta Primavera

Lasagna Loops

*Macaroni Vegetable
Ring Mold*

Pasta & Cabbage

Polenta

Donovan's Rice Bake

Spinach-Rice Casserole

Saffron Rice

Nassau Grits

▼ ▼ ▼

SALADS, RICE & PASTA

▼ ▼ ▼

In preparing salads, your microwave oven comes in very handy for cooking seafood, poultry, meats and other items that are then mixed with the other fresh and cooked ingredients. And in warm weather, when salads are most popular, you won't heat up the kitchen while cooking.

Preparing rice in a microwave oven takes about as long as by conventional cooking. But it won't scorch. And it won't stick to the bottom of the pan, so there's no waste.

Pastas such as spaghetti and fettucini are examples of items that are even more suited to conventional, stovetop cooking than for microwave preparation. Getting the water to a rolling boil in a microwave oven takes more time and energy than on the range, so there's no real benefit to using your microwave oven.

However, larger pastas—particularly lasagne—will stay flat, uncurled and separated when cooked by microwave. Even though there's no time benefit, I cook lasagne in the microwave because it's easier.

▼ ▼ ▼

Hot Shrimp Salad

TO SERVE 4

1 pound large shrimp
(16 to 21 count), peeled
and deveined
½ cup lemon juice
1 tablespoon olive oil
1 tablespoon soy sauce
1 bunch romaine lettuce,
torn into pieces
1 grapefruit, peeled,
seeded and cut into
1-inch pieces
1 can (11 oz.) mandarin
oranges
1 small red onion,
thinly sliced

Sauce

Juice from shrimp
Juice from oranges
2 teaspoons cornstarch

Some recipes are truly amazing in their simplicity and elegance. Here's an example I particularly like.

1. Place shrimp, lemon juice, olive oil and soy sauce in 2-quart ring pan. Cover and cook at 100% power (high) for 5 to 7 minutes or until shrimp are just done and have turned pink. Set aside.
2. Drain juice into a small bowl. Add juice from oranges and whisk in cornstarch. Cook, uncovered, at 100% power for 2 to 3 minutes or until thickened.
3. Meanwhile, place lettuce, grapefruit, oranges and onion in salad bowl and toss.
4. Add shrimp to salad, spoon over sauce and toss.

▼ ▼ ▼

Red Potato Salad

TO SERVE 4

12 small red potatoes
½ cup plain yogurt
2 tablespoons mustard
Lemon pepper
½ cup chopped parsley
Salt and freshly
ground pepper

The flavor of these little potatoes is fantastic.

1. Place unpeeled potatoes in bowl with 1/2 cup water. Cover and cook at 100% power (high) for 8 to 10 minutes. Poke with a fork to determine doneness. Pour off water. Add yogurt, mustard, lemon pepper, chopped parsley and salt and pepper to taste.
2. Serve warm, at room temperature or chilled.

▼ ▼ ▼

Potato Salad

TO SERVE 4

2 medium Idaho potatoes

1 cup water

½ cup mayonnaise

2 tablespoon prepared mustard

2 eggs, hard cooked and diced

1 medium onion, chopped

1 tablespoon dill weed

2 tablespoons capers (optional)

Parsley sprigs for garnish

Potato salad is an essential part of the American cuisine and there are an infinite number of variations. This is my particular favorite. By adding water when cooking the potatoes, they're moister. This is desirable both for slicing and for texture.

1. Choose the best quality potatoes you can find. Place potatoes, peeled or unpeeled, and water in a 1-quart casserole dish, cover and cook at 100% power (high) for about 8 minutes. The water results in a moister potato, which is desirable both for slicing and texture. Cool and dice the potatoes.

2. Add mayonnaise, mustard, eggs, onion, dill weed and capers, if desired. Mix together and serve. Garnish with parsley.

▼ ▼ ▼

Egg Salad with Watercress

TO SERVE 4

6 large eggs

1 bunch watercress, (leaves only) chopped (about 1 cup)

2 scallions, sliced thinly

½ cup mayonnaise

½ cup plain yogurt

Small Romaine lettuce leaves

As this recipe demonstrates, a microwave muffin pan can be used for many things in addition to muffins.

1. Place 1 tablespoon water in each cup of muffin pan. Crack an egg in each cup. Cover with plastic wrap. Cook at 70% (medium-high) about 5 minutes or until eggs are hard cooked.

2. Remove eggs from muffin pan. Chop and mix with watercress, scallions, mayonnaisse and yogurt.

3. Arrange Romaine leaves on individual salad plates. Place a small amount of salad on each and garnish with rolled-up slices of meat and cheese, a few olives and a sprig of watercress.

Warm Lamb Salad with Peanut and Black Currant Dressing

TO SERVE 4

- 1 pound lamb loin or a piece of leg roast trimmed of all fat
  MicroShake or other browning agent (optional)
- 1 head bibb or butter lettuce
- ¼ cup dry roasted peanuts
- ¼ cup raisins
- 4 leaves radicchio
- 4 leaves arugula
- 1 ripe tomato, quartered

Dressing

- 2 tablespoon black currant jelly
- 1 tablespoon Dijon mustard
- 1½ tablespoon red wine vinegar
  Salt and freshly ground pepper
- ½ teaspoon minced fresh thyme leaves
- ½ cup peanut oil

When Chef Dennis Clews to American from Australia, he brought with him a style of cooking that makes Aussie dishes so distinctive. As a guest on my show, he introduced me to some interesting twists in the preparation of lamb and seafood. For a great lunch dish when entertaining special friends, I heartily recommend this recipe.

1. Coat lamb with browning agent, if desired. Place on roasting rack and cook, uncovered, at 70% power (medium-high) for 7 to 8 minutes, or until meat reaches 140 degrees. Set aside.

2. Whisk together currant jelly, mustard, vinegar and thyme. Slowly whisk in oil and then season to taste with salt and freshly ground pepper. Slice thinly. Break up lettuce and mix with other ingredients.

3. Tear up lettuce into bite-sized pieces and mix with peanuts, raisins and other greens. Arrange salad on large place and on large plate and top with sliced lamb. Cook, uncovered, at 100% power (high) for 1 minute.

4. Spoon some of the dressing over the salad. Garnish with tomato and pass remaining dressing at the table.

▼ ▼ ▼

Pasta Primavera

TO SERVE 6

- 2 small zucchini, sliced
- 1½ cups broccoli flowerets
- 6 stalks asparagas, sliced
- 10 mushrooms, quartered
- 1 cup sliced green beans
- 1 cup fresh (or frozen) peas
- 8 ounces whole-wheat spaghetti or soba pasta
- 1 tablespoon extra-virgin olive oil
- 2 cloves garlic, minced
- ¼ teaspoon crushed red pepper flakes
- ¼ cup salt-free chicken broth, defatted
- ¼ cup chopped fresh basil or 1 tablespoon Italian herbs
- 12 cherry tomatoes, halved
- ¼ cup minced Italian parsley
- 2 tablespoon grated Parmesan cheese

Harriet Roth suggests seasonal vegetables as a sauce for pasta. But she says, be careful not to overcook.

1. Place zuchini, broccoli, asparagas, mushrooms, beans and peas in steamer inside 3-quart casserole dish. Cook at 100% power (high) for 5 to 7 minutes or until vegetables are crisp, yet tender.

2. In the meantime, cook pasta in boiling water on the stovetop for 8 to 10 minutes or until al dente. Drain.

3. Place oil and garlic in 1½-quart cook-and-measure bowl and cook at 100% power (high), uncovered, for 3 to 4 minutes. Stir in red pepper, broth, basil, vegetables and tomatoes.

4. Arrange hot pasta on large platter and spoon over vegetable mixture. Garnish with minced parsley and sprinkle with cheese.

From DELICIOUSLY SIMPLE: *Quick-and-Easy Low Sodium, Low-Fat, Low-Cholesterol, Low-Sugar Meals* by Harriet Roth. Copyright 1986 by Harriet Roth. Reprinted by arrangement with NAL PEGUIN INC., New York, NY.

▼ ▼ ▼

Lasagna Loops

Instead of serving lasagna noodles in the traditional layered way, try making these "loops" for an interesting and unique presentation.

TO SERVE 4

10 dry lasagna noodles
 5 Italian sausages (about 1 lb.), cut in 2-inch pieces
 1 cup chopped onions
 2 tablespoon minced garlic
 2 tablespoon spaghetti sauce seasoning
 1 quart fresh or prepared spaghetti sauce

Filling

 1 pint ricotta cheese or low-fat cottage cheese
 1 cup grated mozzarella cheese
 ½ cup grated parmesan cheese
 2 eggs beaten

1. Place lasagna in 9" x 13" cooking pan and cover with water. Cover and cook at 100% power (high) for 10 to 12 minutes or until al dente. Drain.
2. Place sausages in 3-quart casserole fitted with steamer. Cover and cook at 100% power (high) for about 5 minutes. Drain off fat.
3. In cook-and-measure bowl, place onions, garlic and spaghetti seasoning. Cook, uncovered, at 100% power (high) for 3 minutes. Combine with spaghetti sauce.
4. Mix riccota (or low-fat cottage cheese), mozzarella and Parmesan cheeses and eggs thoroughly and spread on each noodle. Place sausage half on noodle and roll up. Position around edge of 9" x 13" baking pan and cover with remaining filling.
5. Cook at 100% power (high), covered, for 8 to 10 minutes or until cheese is melted.

▼ ▼ ▼

Macaroni Vegetable Ring Mold

As I've experimented with dishes over the years, I've come to particularly like the way pasta and vegetables work together. A ring dish such as this is tasty, nutritious and looks great.

TO SERVE 4

 4 cups elbow macaroni, cooked and drained
 1 package (16 oz.) frozen mixed oriental vegetables
 4 eggs
 1½ cups cream
 1 cup grated Parmesan cheese
 3 cups grated mozzarella cheese

1. Place cooked macaroni and vegetables, prepared per directions on package, in 2-quart ring pan.
2. Beat together eggs and cream. Add parmesan and mozzarella cheese.
3. Pour over macaroni, add vegetables and stir together. Cook at 100% power (high), covered, for 8 to 10 minutes or until set.

▼ ▼ ▼

Pasta and Cabbage

TO SERVE 4

6 cups cabbage, chopped

3 Tbsp olive oil

Salt and freshly ground pepper

1 package (16 oz.) bow tie noodles

½ cup heavy cream or condensed milk

½ cup grated Parmesan cheese

Here's a healthy combination: tasty pasta and the flavor and fiber of cabbage. Tastes great, too. Here's a tip to remember when cooking pasta. Make a double amount and keep the extra in your fridge. When you reheat it in your microwave, it's just like fresh-cooked, but without all the work and bother.

1. Place cabbage, oil, salt and pepper in 3-quart casserole dish. Cover and cook at 100% power (high) for 10 minutes.
2. In the meantime, prepare noodles as directed. Drain noodles and add to cooked cabbage.
3. Add cream or condensed milk and Parmesan cheese.

▼ ▼ ▼

Polenta

TO SERVE 4 TO 8

1 cup coarse-ground corn meal

1 quart water

1½ cups grated Parmesan cheese

Pasta isn't the only way Italians incorporate starch in their diet. Polenta is a staple dish commonly served in Italian homes. It's a super-easy, very tasty side dish.

1. Combine corn meal, water and cheese in ring pan. Cook, uncovered, at 70% power (medium-high) for 25 to 30 minutes, stirring occasionally until thick.
2. Set aside to coolk and then refrigerate.
3. Slice and serve, or better yet, fry the slices in a little butter or olive oil. Serve with tomato sauce.

▾ ▾ ▾

Donovan's Rice Bake

TO SERVE 4 TO 6

1 frying chicken (3 to 4 lbs.), cut up

1 package (10 oz.) frozen peas

1 can (16 oz.) stewed tomatoes

1 cup water

4 hot Italian sausages

1 medium onion, chopped

1 green pepper, seeded and chopped

1 red pepper, seeded and chopped

1 tablespoon dried basil

1 cup long grain rice

½ pound shrimp, shelled and deveined

Salt and freshly ground pepper

I really enjoy making one-dish meals in a microwave oven because they're so easy. This particular recipe is similar to the paella of Spanish cuisine. In making this recipe, you'll also see how easy it is to make a simple chicken stock.

1. Remove and reserve chicken skin. To make the stock, place chicken skin, wings and back section in a 2-quart casserole with the water. Cook, covered, at 100% power (high) for 20 minutes.

2. In the meantime, in a 2-quart ring pan, arrange chicken parts around the bottom. Place sausages, onion, green and red peppers, basil and salt and pepper to taste over chicken. Add peas, tomatoes and rice. Measure 1 cup of chicken stock and carefully pour over the top.

3. Cover and cook at 100% power (high) for 30 minutes.

4. Add shrimp, recover, and cook at 100% power (high) for 5 minutes or until shrimp are done.

▾ ▾ ▾

Spinach-Rice Casserole

TO SERVE 4

3 pounds spinach, washed and chopped (or frozen spinach, thawed and squeezed of excess water)

1 bunch scallions, chopped

2 tablespoons dried dill weed

1 cup long-grain rice

1½ cups water or chicken stock

½ cup wheat germ

Cooking rice in a microwave oven takes as long as on top of the stove. But the beauty of microwaving is that you can set it and forget it. Because the microwave turns off automatically after the set time has elapsed and the pot doesn't get hot, you don't have to worry about scorching or burning.

1. Place everything in a 2- or 3-quart ring pan.

2. Cook at 100% power (high), uncovered, for 18 to 20 minutes or until the rice is cooked. If you use brown rice, cook for about 35 to 40 minutes.

**Snow Peas with Herbed Cheese
and Caviar-topped Potatoes**

Dilled Carrot Soup

**Warm Lamb Salad
with Black Currant Dressing**

**Truite au Bleu and Poached Pear
with Raspberry Sauce**

▼ ▼ ▼

Saffron Rice

TO SERVE 4

1 large onion, chopped

¼ teaspoon ground cloves

½ teaspoon ground cinnamon

¼ teaspoon cardamom seeds

1 cup long-grain rice, rinsed (or converted rice)

2 cups water

1 teaspoon saffron threads

3 tablespoon hot water

A little bit more work than ordinary rice. But is it ever worth it.

1. Place the onion, cloves, cinnamon, cardamom and rice in 2-quart ring pan. Cover and cook at 100% power (high) for 3 to 4 minutes.
2. Add water and cook at 100% power (high), uncovered, for 18 to 20 minutes or until water is absorbed and rice is tender.
3. In the meantime, soak the saffron in the hot water. Add the saffron and water to the cooked rice, stirring to blend.

▼ ▼ ▼

Nassau Grits

TO SERVE 4

1 green pepper, chopped

1 medium yellow onion, chopped

1 pound lean baked ham, cut in 1-inch cubes

1 cup quick grits

3 cups water

¼ cup prepared hot sauce

1 can (16 oz.) stewed tomatoes

1 cup imitation bacon bits or 6 slices of bacon, cooked crisp and crumbled

½ cup chopped parsley

On a radio interview, a caller provided me with a recipe for what she called "Nassau Grits." I'd never heard of it before, but it sounded interesting, so I tried it. It's a wonderful and easy-to-make dish. I wish I knew the woman's name, so I could give her credit.

1. Place green pepper, onions and ham in 3-quart casserole dish. Cover and cook at 100% power (high) for 3 to 4 minutes or until vegetables are soft.
2. Add grits, water, hot sauce and tomatoes. Cook at 100% power (high), covered, for 8 to 10 minutes, or until grits are cooked. Add more water if too thick.
3. Top with bacon bits, or real bacon, and parsley to serve.

Seafood

▼

Poached Salmon

Whole Steamed Salmon

Snappy Snapper

Fish Picante

Swordfish Caliente

Haddock in
Cream Sauce

Truite au Bleu

Trout Amondine

Finnan Haddie

Sea Bass in
Black Bean Sauce

Seafood Medley with
Tropical Butter Sauce

Curried Clams

Spicy Clams

Steamed Mussels with
Garlic Butter

▼ ▼ ▼

▼

Oysters & Pepperoni
in Cream

Shrimp Creole Montero

Gumbo

Etoufee

Steamed Lobster

Lobster Thermidor

▼ ▼ ▼

S E A F O O D

▼ ▼ ▼

To poach, steam or sauté fish and shellfish, microwaving is without a doubt the best way to cook.

Both fish and shellfish have high water content, so when you microwave it, you're actually cooking it in its own juices. But sometimes a small amount of poaching liquid—fish stock, clam juice, dry white wine, Japanese miso soup or a little water and herbs—can be used to intensify the flavors.

The two most important rules are: always keep the dish covered; and don't overcook.

Fried or batter-coated fish and shellfish can be done better conventionally. But when you're preparing something as delicate and subtle as fish and shellfish, why bread and fry it in the first place? It's so much better poached or sauteed in your microwave flavored with a little lemon juice and garlic.

▾ ▾ ▾

Poached Salmon

TO SERVE 4

1 cup water

½ cup lemon juice

1 small onion, sliced

4 sprigs fresh parsley or dill

1 stalk celery (with leaves), sliced

6 peppercorns

4 salmon steaks (4 oz. each)

Sprigs of fresh dill for garnish

Thin slices of lemon for garnish

When selecting guests for my television show, we wanted to have someone who emphasized healthy cooking. I found a book by Harriet Roth called, "Deliciously Simple" in which she says, ". . . first consider a microwave." After reading that, I had to have her on the show. Her recipes are wonderful, and if you're interested in eating a healthier diet as well, be sure to buy her book.

When Harriet poaches salmon in a microwave oven, it's simple, tasty, healthful and beautiful.

1. Place water, lemon juice, onion, parsley or dill, celery and peppercorns in 2-quart casserole. Cover and cook at 100% power for 5 to 7 minutes.

2. Place salmon in dish in a single layer, not stacked. Recover and cook at 100% power (high) for 4 to 5 minutes or until salmon reaches 140 degrees and begins to flake.

3. Arrange salmon steaks on individual plates. Garnish each with a small sprig of dill and a few slices of lemon.

From DELICIOUSLY SIMPLE: *Quick-and-Easy Low Sodium, Low-Fat, Low-Cholesterol, Low-Sugar Meals* by Harriet Roth. Copyright 1986 by Harriet Roth. Reprinted by arrangement with NAL PEGUIN INC., New York, NY.

▼ ▼ ▼

Whole Steamed Salmon

TO SERVE 4

2 tablespoons whole
   black peppercorns
½ cup celery, chopped
½ cup onions, chopped
½ cup carrots, chopped
1½ cups dry white wine
1 salmon (about 3 lbs.),
   cleaned

When microwaving any fish this large, be sure you use less than full power. If cooked on full power, sometimes the sides of the fish will burst in spots which spoils the appearance.

1. In a cook-and-measure bowl, combine the peppercorns, celery, onions, carrots and wine. Cook at 100% power (high), uncovered, for 5 minutes.

2. Place salmon in a 9"x13" casserole dish in an upright position with the belly flaps open and down. Spoon wine and vegetable mixture over the fish. Cover with plastic wrap. Cook at 70% power (medium-high) for 12 to 15 minutes or until temperature of fish in thickest part reaches 150 degrees.

Snappy Snapper

TO SERVE 4

4 fillets of red snapper, cod, bass or rockfish (about 4 oz. each)

1 bunch scallions, thinly sliced

¼ cup prepared hot sauce

True red snapper is found in tropical or semitropical waters. Often what is sold as snapper is actually a rockfish and not a snapper at all. But don't worry about this ichthyological knit-picking. Either will work beautifully.

1. Brush both sides of the fish with hot sauce. (Tabasco sauce is too hot for this dish, so use a milder version.)
2. Place in 1-quart casserole dish and top with scallions. Cover and cook at 100% power (high) for 4 to 6 minutes or until fish is done (150 degrees). Check underside of fish to be sure it's cooked completely.

Fish Picante

TO SERVE 4

1 medium onion, sliced

2 cloves garlic, minced

¼ cup cilantro stems, chopped

4 fillets of cod, halibut or shark (4 oz. each)

1½ cups picante sauce

¼ teaspoon ground cinnamon

8 pimento-stuffed green olives, sliced
Cilantro leaves

Many recipes call for a long list of individual ingredients: 1/4 tsp of this, 1/8 cup of that and a smidgen of something else. Often, you can achieve the same authentic flavor using a prepared sauce. That's what I've done here by substituting prepared picante sauce.

1. Place onions, garlic and cilantro stems in a shallow 1-quart casserole. Cover and cook at 100% power (high) for 3 minutes.
2. Add the fish, pour sauce over and srinkle on cinnamon. Recover and cook at 100% power (high) for 6 to 8 minutes or until the fish flakes or reaches 150 degrees.
3. Garnish with olives and cilantro leaves.

▼ ▼ ▼

Swordfish Caliente

TO SERVE 4

4 shark steaks (about 4
oz. each)
Garlic and chilli paste
(available at Asian
food stores) or the
home-made sauce
below
½ cup cilantro, chopped

Sauce

5 garlic cloves 1
tablespoon 3
1 tablespoon sesame oil
1 tablespoon flour
1 tablespoon lemon
juice
Process or mash until
smooth and blended.

Swordfish steaks are firm and delicate. This spicy recipe uses ingredients from a variety ethnic cuisines in a tasty combination. If swordfish isn't available, you can use shark or any large-flaked fish such as halibut, cod or snapper.

1. Place fish in 3-quart casserole dish or appropriately sized rectangular glass dish.
2. Process sauce ingredients until smooth and spread over fish.
3. Cover and cook at 100% (high) for 4 to 6 minutes or until fish is done. Garnish with cilantro.

▾ ▾ ▾   # Haddock in Cream Sauce

TO SERVE 4

1 pound haddock fillets
1 cup milk
1 teaspoon fennel seeds, crushed
2 tablespoon flour
2 tablespoon butter
Freshly ground pepper
¼ cup minced parsley

Found in North Atlantic waters, the haddock is related to the cod. It's generally reasonable in price, and popular for its firm, white meat.

1. Place fish on the sides of a 1-quart casserole dish.
2. Add the milk and fennel seeds. Cover and cook at 100% power (high) for 5 to 6 minutes or until fish reaches 150 degrees. Set aside.
3. In a 1½-quart cook-and-measure bowl, combine the flour and butter and cook, uncovered, at 100% power (high) for 1 to 1½ minutes.
4. Pour in poaching liquid and cook at 100% power (high) for 1 to 3 minutes or until thickened.
5. Transfer haddock to a serving platter and spoon over the sauce. Sprinkle with pepper and minced parsley to serve.

Truite au Bleu

▼ ▼ ▼

TO SERVE 2

½ cup water
½ cup tarragon vinegar
1 teaspoon kosher salt
¼ teaspoon freshly ground black pepper
1 whole brook, brown or rainbow trout (14 to 16 oz.)
Slivers of lemon peel
Fresh tarragon for garnish

When Barbara Kafka was a guest on my show, she prepared this delicious trout for me. The fish cooks in an acidic poaching liquid that causes the skin to turn blue, hence the name. Barbara noted that frozen trout work well when cooked in the microwave this way.

1. Combine water, vinegar, salt and pepper in 13½" x 9½" x 2" dish. Heat, uncovered, at 100% power (high) for 8 minutes.
2. Remove from oven. Slip the trout into the hot liquid. Cover tightly with microwave plastic wrap. Cook at 100% power (high) for 2 minutes. Remove from oven, uncover and carefully turn the fish over. Recover and cook at 100% power (high) for 2 additional minutes.
3. Uncover and transfer fish with a wide metal spatula to a serving plate. Garnish with slivers of lemon peel and fresh tarragon leaves.

Original recipe appears in Barbara Kafka's *Microwave Gourmet,* published by William Morrow and Company, Inc., 1987.

▾ ▾ ▾   # Trout Amondine

TO SERVE 4

4 small trout (about
6 oz. each)

½ cup slivered almonds

2 tablespoons lemon
juice

2 tablespoons butter

4 slices bacon,
microwaved crisp and
crumbled

4 tablespoons parsley,
chopped

Whoever came up with the idea of using sliced
almonds with trout deserves some sort of medal. This
is a truly perfect combination of flavors.

1. Place bacon on microwave broiling rack or plate.
    Cover with paper towel to prevent spattering.
    Cook at 100% power (high) for 3 1/2 minutes.
    Check for doneness and cook additionally, if
    necessary. Set aside.

2. Place trout, head to tail, around the edges of a
    3-quart, rectangular microwave cooking dish.
    Position them upright with the belly flaps
    spread open.

3. Cover and cook at 70% power (medium-high) for
    8 to 10 minutes.

4. Transfer fish to a serving platter and keep warm.
    Pour poaching liquid into a bowl and stir in
    almonds, lemon juice and butter.

5. Cook, uncovered at 100% power (high) for
    2 minutes. Pour over fish and garnish with
    bacon and parsley to serve.

Finnan Haddie

TO SERVE 4

4 fillets (about 1 lb.)
  Finnan Haddie
  Milk
4 pats butter (about 1 oz.
  each), room
  temperature
  Freshly ground pepper

Finnan Haddie is a Scottish term for smoked haddock. It's a bit salty, but I think it's delicious. The first time I had it was for breakfast in London. I still make it for breakfast from time to time. Nutritionally, it's high in protein and low in fat.

1. Place fillets around the sides of a shallow 1-quart casserole dish. Add enough milk to just cover the fish.
2. Cover and cook at 100% power (high) for 6 to 8 minutes or until the fish flakes apart easily. (Note: The starting temperature of the milk will directly affect how long this dish will take to cook. If the milk is right out of the refrigerator and very cold, add a little to the cooking time. The times indicated assume milk at room temperature.)
3. Pour off milk. Transfer fish to a serving platter and top each with a pat of butter and ground pepper.

Sea Bass in Black Bean Sauce

TO SERVE 4

¼ cup black bean sauce
1 tablespoon soy sauce
2 tablespoons shredded
  ginger root (or ginger
  paste)
2 tablespoons dry sherry
1 whole sea bass (about
  1 lb.) or 4 pieces sea
  bass (about 4 oz. each)
4 scallions, thinly sliced

If you check your Chinese cookbooks, you'll find the fish in the recipe is always steamed. Anytime you see a recipe that requires steaming, make it in your microwave because it's so much easier than on the stove top.

1. Mix bean sauce, soy sauce, ginger and sherry. Paint onto both sides of fish and place in shallow 1-quart casserole.
2. Cover and cook at 100% power (high) 4 to 6 minutes or until fish flakes easily or reaches 150 degrees.
3. Garnish with sliced scallions to serve.

▾ ▾ ▾

Seafood Medley with Tropical Butter Sauce

TO SERVE 4

- 1 small shallot, chopped
- 1 small clove garlic, minced
- ¼ cup dry white wine
- ¼ cup clam juice
- 6 green-lip (New Zealand) mussels (or 12 local mussels), scrubbed
- 4 large shrimp, peeled and deveined
- 8 large roe-on Tasmanian scallops or 8 large local scallops
- 4 tablespoons heavy cream
- ¼ pound butter
- 1 passion fruit, pulp only
- 1 slice mango, (about 1-inch thick), chopped
- 1 tablespoon chopped chives
- 1 tablespoon cornstarch, mixed with 2 tablespoons water

Not all of the ingredients for Dennis Clews' Australian specialties are readily available around the U.S. So I've indicated alternatives for some of the harder-to-find items in this delectable dish. But ask your grocer before you make the change.

1. Combine shallot, garlic, wine and clam juice in a 3-quart casserole dish. Cover and cook at 100% (high) for 3 minutes.

2. Add mussels, recover and cook at 100% power (high) for 2 to 3 minutes or until all the mussels are open. (Discard any mussels that don't open.)

3. Remove the cooked mussels and set aside.

4. Add shrimp, scallops, cream, butter, passion fruit and mango. Cover, cook at 100% power (high) for 3 to 4 minutes or until shrimp are pink.

5. Pour juices into 1½-quart cook-and-measure bowl. Whisk in cornstarch mixture and cook at 100% power (high), uncovered, for 1 to 2 minutes or until thickened.

6. Place seafood on a decorative serving platter. Tuck mussels in alongside. Spoon over the sauce and garnish with chives.

▼ ▼ ▼   # Curried Clams

2 dozen small cherrystone (or little neck) clams

½ cup dry white wine or water

2 tablespoon oil (optional)

¼ cup fresh ginger, shredded

4 tablespoon garlic, minced

2 tablespoon curry powder

1 teaspoon dried chilli flakes

4 tablespoon fresh coriander stems, chopped

1 tablespoon lemon juice

4 tablespoon fresh coriander leaves, chopped

½ cup shredded raw coconut

Hot cooked rice

This dish will have your friends asking for the recipe.

1. Place clams and wine in a 3-quart casserole dish. Tuck foil around and over the clams. Cover with dish cover or plastic wrap. Cook at 100% power (high) for 8 to 12 minutes or until all clams are open. Discard any clams that don't open.

2. Drain juices into cook-and-measure bowl and add oil, ginger, garlic, curry powder, chilli flakes, coriander stems and lemon. Cook, uncovered, at 100% power (high) for 3 minutes.

3. Pour over clams and mix in coriander leaves and coconut.

4. Serve over rice.

▾ ▾ ▾   ## Spicy Clams

TO SERVE 4

2 dozen small
cherrystone (or little
neck) clams, scrubbed

½ cup dry white wine or
water

½ cup lemon juice

¼ cup butter or oil

¼ cup prepared hot
sauce (not Tabasco)

4 cloves garlic, minced

¼ cup shredded fresh
ginger

1 tablespoon chilli and
garlic paste

Cajun-style cooking is particularly well-suited to seafood as this clam recipe demonstrates. The chilli and garlic paste is available at Asian markets. Also, the reason for not using Tabasco sauce is its intense hotness. It's great for many uses, but not here.

1. Place clams, wine and lemon juice in 2-quart ring pan. Tuck foil around and over the clams. Cover with plastic wrap. Cook at 100% power (high) for 8 to 10 minutes or until all clams are open. (Discard any clams that don't open.)
2. Drain 1 cup of clam broth into cook-and-measure bowl. (Save the rest for other fish recipes. Freeze it and it'll keep.)
3. Add butter or oil, hot sauce, garlic, ginger and chilli and garlic paste to the broth. Stir and cook at 100% power (high) for 3 minutes. Pour sauce over clams or use it for dipping.

Steamed Mussels with Garlic Butter

¼ **pound butter**
4 **large garlic cloves, minced**
¼ **cup parsley, chopped**
Freshly ground pepper

Mussels are relatively inexpensive for shellfish. I happen to think they're delicious and encourage people to serve them more often, particularly in view of their nutritional value. Compared to 3.5 oz. of beef, 3.5 oz. of mussels have less than ¼ the calories, the same amount of protein, about 1/20th the fat, 5 times more calcium, and ⅓ more phosphorus, iron, and riboflavin.

1. Wash and scrub 2 dozen mussels. Cook as described on opposite page for clams. Then dip the steamed mussels in this garlic butter.
2. Heat in a 2-cup serving dish for 1 to 1½ minutes.
3. Serve with French or sour-dough bread.

Oysters and Pepperoni in Cream

TO SERVE 4

3 **ounces pepperoni, chopped**
1 **jar (10 oz.) fresh oysters and juice**
1 **cup cream**
¼ **cup flour**

Usually this recipe is made with Cajun sausage called Tasso. Since it's not available most places, I've substituted pepperoni, which is available everywhere.

1. Place pepperoni in 2-quart casserole dish. Cover, and cook at 100% (high) for 2 minutes.
2. Add oysters, cream and flour. Cook at 100% power (high), uncovered, for 2 to 3 minutes until oysters are cooked and cream thickens.
3. Serve over buttered rusks or cooked rice.

Shrimp Creole Montero

▾ ▾ ▾

½ cup flour

½ cup oil

1 medium yellow onion, chopped

1 small stalk celery, chopped

1 scallion, thinly sliced

6 cloves garlic, minced

¼ cup chopped parsley

1 can (4 oz.) tomato sauce

1 cup water

2 pounds uncooked shrimp, peeled and deveined

Salt and freshly ground pepper

Cayene pepper

This recipe was offered by my good friend George Montero, a native of New Orleans who introduced me to that wonderful city.

1. Place the flour and oil in heat-proof glass, 4-cup measuring bowl. Cook at 100% power (high), uncovered, for 6 to 7 minutes or until the roux is a dark caramel color, stirring in 1-minute increments after the first 3 to 4 minutes. (Be careful not to burn the flour and remember the bowl will be very hot.)

2. Stir in the onions, celery, and scallions and cook at 100% power (high) for 3 minutes.

3. Add garlic and parsley and cook 2 minutes more. Pour mixture into 3-quart casserole dish. Stir in the tomato sauce, water and seasonings. Cover and cook at 100% power (high) for 5 minutes.

4. Add shrimp, cover and cook at 100% power (high) for about 10 minutes, stirring once, or until shrimp are cooked.

▼ ▼ ▼

Gumbo

TO SERVE 4

¼ cup oil

¼ cup flour

2 medium onions, chopped

1 package (10 oz.) frozen okra, thawed and cut into 1/2-inch pieces

1 pound Cajun or hot Italian sausage

2 cans (10 oz.) tomatoes and chilies or 1/4 cup diced hot chilies and 1 can (15 oz.) stewed tomatoes

¼ cup prepared hot sauce

1 pound shrimp (small to medium), peeled and deveined

Ever wonder where the name "gumbo" comes from? In the Bantu language of Africa, it means "okra", so be sure not to leave that ingredient out. Otherwise, it just won't be gumbo.

Also, it's important to use heat-proof glass bowls where indicated. The roux generates a great deal of heat during cooking and may damage other cookware.

1. Place oil and flour in 2-quart heat-proof glass bowl. Cook at 100% power (high) for 3 to 5 minutes, stirring every minute until the roux begins to brown. Be careful not to burn. Reduce cooking time to 15 seconds toward end to control browning. A tan color will provide mild flavor, whereas a dark brown will have a very intense aroma.

2. Stir onions and okra into roux. Cover and cook at 100% (high) for 5 to 8 minutes or until onions are soft. Set aside.

3. Cook sausage in a 3-quart casserole with a steamer at 100% power (high) for 5 minutes. Remove the steamer insert and discard fat.

4. Place cooked okra, onions and sausage, along with tomatoes and chilies, hot sauce and shrimp in 3-quart casserole. Cook at 100% power (high), covered, for 5 to 7 minutes or until shrimp are just cooked and have turned pink.

5. In the meantime, heat 1 quart of water on the stove top. Carefully add to gumbo mix and stir. Serve with rice or grits.

▼ ▼ ▼

Etoufée

TO SERVE 4

¼ pound butter
½ cup flour
1 medium green pepper, chopped
1 large stalk celery, chopped
1 bunch scallions, chopped
1½ pounds crayfish meat
1 can (10 oz.) tomatoes and chillis (or 1 can stewed tomatoes)
1 cup Bloody Mary mix Tabasco

There are as many variations of this Cajun dish as there are Cajun cooks. Try this and then make up your own. For example substitute uncooked shrimp, scallops, lobster, raw cubed turkey breast or any combination for the crayfish.

1. Place butter, flour, green pepper, celery and scallions in 3-quart casserole. Cook, covered, at 100% power (high) for 3 to 4 minutes or until vegetables are soft.
2. Stir in crayfish (or other seafood and meat), tomatoes and chillis, Bloody Mary mix and Tabasco to taste. Cover and cook at 100% (high) for 8 to 10 minutes or until seafood or meat is just cooked, 150 degrees. Stir once and add more Bloody Mary mix if too thick.
3. Serve over rice or pasta.

▼ ▼ ▼

Steamed Lobster

TO SERVE 4

4 lobsters (about 1–1 1/4 lbs. each, called "chicks")
1 cup dry white wine or water

It used to be only New Englanders could enjoy fresh lobster. Now they're available around the country. Even though they're expensive, indulge yourself occasionally with this succulent and richly flavored delicacy of the sea. Here's a quick and humane way to prepare lobster for cooking. With a knife, make a crosswise cut just behind its head, at the first shell joint. This instantly kills the lobster.

1. Place lobsters in a 9" x 13" baking dish.
2. Heat the wine at 100% power (high) in a measuring cup for 2 minutes.
3. Pour over lobsters and cover with plastic wrap. Cook at 100% power (high) for about 4 minutes per lobster or until they turn pink.

▼ ▼ ▼

Lobster Thermidor

TO SERVE 4

4 steamed lobsters
(1 to 1 1/4 lb. each)

2 cups sliced
mushrooms

1 bunch scallions, sliced

2 tablespoons butter

1 tablespoon
Worcestershire sauce

1 teaspoon Tabasco

½ cup sweet sherry

2 cups cream or
condensed milk

½ cup shopped parsley

½ cup grated Parmesan
cheese

2 tablespoons flour
mixed with 3
tablespoons water
Parsley sprigs

This old classic does very well by microwave. You may want to place it under the broiler just before serving to give it a more traditional appearance.

1. Break off legs from lobster and save. Remove meat from tail and claws and cut into 1-inch pieces.
2. Place mushrooms, scallions, butter, Worcestershire sauce, Tabasco and sherry in 1½-quart cook-and-measure bowl. Cook at 100% power (high), covered, for 5 minutes.
3. Add cream or condensed milk, parsley, Parmesan cheese, flour and water, and lobster meat. Cook at 100% power (high), uncovered, for 3 to 5 minutes or until thickened. Add lobster and spoon into individual serving dishes.
4. Garnish each with reserved lobster legs and a sprig of parsley.

Poultry

▼

Southern Baked Chicken

Stuffed Roaster

Chicken & Apples
with Yogurt

Chicken Fricassee

Naked Chicken Stuffed
with Frozen Vegetables

Chicken Matzoh
Casserole

Indonesian Chicken
with Peanut Sauce

Chicken on a Bed
of Peppers

Sherried Chicken Legs

Chicken Mole

Chicken Curry

Brandied Chicken
Breasts

Spicy, Cheesy
Chicken Breasts

▼ ▼ ▼

▼

Chicken Cacciatora

Chicken Potenza

Barbeque Chicken

Chicken Florentine

Taco Turkey Wings

Pickled Chicken
or Turkey

Cornish Hens

Microduck Sauté

▼ ▼ ▼

P O U L T R Y

▼ ▼ ▼

All forms of poultry are very well suited to microwave preparation.

To substantially reduce the fat and cholesterol, remove the skin before cooking in your microwave. It won't dry out as it would in a conventional oven.

Whole chickens by microwave are always tender and juicy. But when you cook smaller portions, such as breasts, they cook so quickly that they don't have time to tenderize. That's why I add a little liquid such as stock, wine, milk or juice and cook it slightly longer so they'll be moist and tender.

Turkey microwaves beautifully. It's not only quicker and easier than by conventional oven, I honestly believe it's better. To be perfectly browned with a crispy skin, finish off the cooking in your conventional oven.

▼ ▼ ▼   Southern Baked Chicken

TO SERVE 4

1 fryer (3 to 4 lbs.),
  cut up
½ cup flour
½ cup plain bread
  crumbs
1 tablespoon
  Micro Shake or
  paprika
  Salt and pepper to
  taste

Gravy

1 cup cream
2 tablespoon flour

Everyone knows about the famous southern fried chicken. Since you can't fry in a microwave oven, here's a recipe for southern baked chicken. You may substitute 1 cup condensed milk for the cream. For a lower-calorie gravy, use 1 cup skim milk in place of cream.

1. Remove back and wing tips and cut chicken into easy-to-eat pieces.
2. Mix flour, bread crumbs and spices. Coat chicken pieces.
3. Arrange chicken in 2-quart ring pan or 3-quart casserole dish. Cover with waxed paper and cook at 50% power (medium), for about 30 minutes. (For extra crispy chicken, place under preheated broiler for 5 minutes after microwave cooking.)
4. Drain off juices from chicken.
5. For gravy, add cream and flour to juices. Cook at 100% power (high) until thick, about 2 to 3 minutes. Pour over chicken to serve.

▼ ▼ ▼   Stuffed Roaster

1 roasting chicken (6 to 8
  lbs.)
  MicroShake browning
  agent
1 box prepared stuffing
  mix

So simple, so good, and it feeds the whole family.

1. Prepare stuffing mix following package directions.
2. Stuff and truss the bird. Coat generously with Micro Shake.
3. Place on a 9" x 13" roasting rack and cover with wax paper.
4. Cook at 70% power (medium-high) for about 45 minutes or to a temperature of 170 degrees.

▼ ▼ ▼

Chicken & Apples with Yogurt

TO SERVE 4

1 large yellow onion, sliced

½ cup apple juice concentrate

½ teaspoon ground nutmeg

1 frying chicken (3 to 4 lbs.), skinned and cut up

2 large crisp apples

1 cup plain yogurt

The fresh-fruit taste of apples and the tang of yogurt are a very palate-pleasing combination.

1. Place onion, apple juice and nutmeg in 3-quart casserole dish. Cover and cook at 10% (high) for 3 to 4 minutes.

2. Add chicken, recover and cook at 100% power (high) for 20 to 25 minutes or until chicken reaches a temperature of 170 degrees.

3. Stir in apples and yogurt. Recover and cook at 100% power (high) for 5 minutes.

▼ ▼ ▼

Chicken Fricassee

TO SERVE 4

1 frying chicken (3 to 4 lbs.), skinned and cut up

4 tablespoons butter

1 cup milk

2 tablespoons flour

"Fricassee" is a French word that means to "cut up and fry". But somehow over time, it's come to mean this creamy way to prepare chicken.

1. Arrange chicken in a ring pan. Add 2 tablespoons of the butter, cut in pieces, and pour over milk.

2. Cover and cook at 100% power (high) for 18 to 20 minutes. Drain off and save juices.

3. Combine remaining 2 tablespoons butter with flour in a cook-and-measure bowl. Add reserved pan juices and stir.

4. Cook, stirring once or twice, at 100% power (high) for 3 to 4 minutes until thick.

5. Pour over chicken to serve.

Naked Chicken Stuffed With Frozen Vegetables

▼ ▼ ▼

TO SERVE 4

1 pound frozen mixed vegetables, thawed

1 frying chicken (3 to 4 lbs.), skinned

½ cup bread crumbs

1 teaspoon dried Italian herbs

¼ teaspoon cayenne pepper

½ teaspoon lemon pepper

This recipe gives you an entire balanced meal of animal protein coupled with a stimulating variety of vegetables all cooked in the fresh, natural chicken juices. Use curry powder and/or five-spice seasoning for a little variety. Like your microwave oven, frozen vegetables save you time.

1. Cook vegetables at 100% power (high), covered, for 5 minutes. When cool enough to handle, stuff vegetables into the cavity of the chicken.
2. Mix together bread crumbs, herbs and pepper. Sprinkle onto the surface of the chicken, pressing gently.
3. Place chicken on a roasting rack or in a cooker-steamer and cover securely with plastic wrap or the dish cover.
4. Cook at 100% power (high) for 20 to 25 minutes or until chicken reaches 180 degrees.

Chicken Matzoh Casserole

▼ ▼ ▼

TO SERVE 4

1 cup onion, chopped

1 tablespoon butter

3 cups cooked chicken, chopped

6 eggs

2 cups chicken stock

1 tablespoon Vegetable Delight seasoning (optional)

2 tablespoons dried dill weed

3 matzoh squares, crumbled

Matzoh is a crisp, unleavened bread that is a staple in Jewish cuisine. It's available anywhere and is usually eaten just like any other bread. But it also happens to be useful as an ingredient in this simple casserole.

1. Cook onion and butter at 100% power (high) for 3 minutes in a small bowl.
2. Mix together chicken, eggs, chicken stock, seasonings and matzohs.
3. Place in 1-quart square casserole dish.
4. Cook at 70% power (medium-high), uncovered, for about 10 minutes or until casserole is set.

▾ ▾ ▾

Indonesian Chicken with Peanut Sauce

TO SERVE 4

2 hot, red chillies, seeded and chopped (or 1 tablespoon dried chilli flakes)

1 large onion, chopped

4 cloves garlic, chopped

1 tablespoon oil

1 teaspoon ground coriander

1 stalk lemon grass (available at Asian food stores) or 1 teaspoon dried lemon peel

1 cup coconut milk

1 tablespoon sugar

2 tablespoons soy sauce

½ cup chunky peanut butter

1 chicken (3 to 4 lbs.), cut up skinned or 4 large chicken breasts

2 tablespoons lemon juice

Tabasco or other prepared hot sauce

Broaden your dining experience by making this recipe. You'll love it. One of the most requested recipes from my TV appearances is African chicken, which also uses peanut butter and chillies. This recipe is even better.

1. Place chillies, onion, garlic, oil, coriander and lemon grass in 3-quart casserole dish or 2-quart ring pan.

2. Cover and cook at 100% power (high) for 3 to 4 minutes.

3. Add coconut milk, sugar, soy sauce, peanut butter and chicken. Recover and cook at 100% power (high) for 20 to 25 minutes or to a temperature of 170 degrees.

4. Stir in lemon juice. Taste for hotness and adjust flavor by adding Tabasco or other prepared hot sauce to taste.

▾ ▾ ▾

Chicken on a Bed of Peppers

1 frying chicken (4 lbs.), cut up or 4 large breasts

1 each red, yellow and green bell pepper, cored and sliced into 1/2-inch-wide pieces

1 large red onion, sliced

4 cloves garlic, chopped

4 tablespoons tomato paste

½ cup dry white wine

4 tablespoons paprika

A beautiful dish that creates a wonderful presentation at a party. Make it when there's an abundance of multi-colored peppers available at a reasonable price.

1. Place chicken in 3-quart casserole dish.
2. Mix peppers, onion, garlic, tomato paste, wine and paprika and pour over chicken.
3. Cover securely with plastic wrap and cook 100% power (high) for 25 to 30 minutes, or until the chicken reaches 170 degrees.

▾ ▾ ▾

Sherried Chicken Legs

4 chicken legs and thighs, skinned

Marinade

½ cup soy sauce

½ cup sweet sherry

1 tablespoon ground ginger

1 tablespoon cornstarch mixed with 2 tablespoons water

Sherry and soy sauce blend together beautifully. The alcohol in the wine cooks off leaving the pleasantly sweet and grapey taste.

1. Place chicken in 2-quart ring pan. Mix marinade ingredients and pour over chicken.
2. Cover and let stand for and hour or so.
3. Cook at 100% power (high) for 15 to 20 minutes, or to a temperature of 170 degrees.
4. Pour off juices and add cornstarch mixture.
5. Stir together and cook at 100% power (high) for 1 minute, or until thickened. Pour over chicken to serve.

▼ ▼ ▼

Chicken Molé

1 small carrot, sliced

1 medium onion, quartered

3 cloves garlic, smashed and peeled

1 cup canned, chopped tomatoes

¼ teaspoon ground cinnamon

¼ teaspoon cumin

¼ teaspoon corriander

¼ teaspoon ground cloves

¼ teaspoon anise

½ teaspoon dried pepper flakes

3 tablespoons oil

¼ cup raisins

3 tablespoons cocoa

1 frying chicken (4 lbs.)

¼ cup toasted sesame seeds

¼ cup slivered almonds

4 pineapple slices

1 orange, peeled and cut into sections

In preparing this recipes, a 4-pound roaster or fryer will serve 4 people. But if you're having a party or larger gathering, use a 10-pound turkey or a 5-pound turkey breast. Use the same amount of sauce for the turkey as you would for the fryer.

1. Place carrot, onion and garlic in 1-quart casserole dish or a 1½-quart cook-and-measure bowl. Cover and cook at 100% power (high) for 3 to 4 minutes. Add tomatoes, cinnamon, cumin, corriander, cloves, anise, pepper flakes, oil, raisins and cocoa and use food processor to blend.

2. Loosen chicken skin by inserting plastic spatula handle or similar tool under the skin and moving it around all parts of the bird. Go in from the neck to loosen skin of the back, and from the cavity opening to loosen breast skin.

3. With the chicken placed in the cooking dish, spoon the sauce under the skin and massage it around so it fills all parts of the bird. Pour the remaining sauce over the bird.

4. Cover the dish with a lid or plastic wrap and cook at 100% power (high) for 15 minutes.

5. Turn bird, recover, and cook at 100% power (high) for 10 to 15 minutes longer, or until the chicken reaches 170 degrees.

6. Place the bird on a serving platter. Remove fat from sauce and pour over bird.

7. Sprinkle with sesame seeds and almonds. Garnish with pineapple and orange sections.

▾ ▾ ▾   # Chicken Curry

TO SERVE 4

1 large onion, chopped

4 cloves garlic, chopped

4 tablespoons grated
fresh ginger

1 teaspoon each ground
cumin, turmeric,
corriander, cayenne
pepper and crushed
fennel seeds

1 frying chicken (3 to 4
lbs.), cut up and
skinned or 4 large
breasts, skinned and
boned

1 can (15 oz.) stewed
tomatoes

½ cup plain yogurt

1 tablespoon garam
marsala (an Indian
spice, optional)

1 tablespoon lemon
juice

Fresh corriander

The more you try curries, the more you'll like curries.
There's such a variety—some hot, some not. All cook
beautifully by microwave. You'll see this recipe
doesn't call for packaged curry powder. As in Indian
kitchens, you'll make your own by using this fragrant
and savory blend of spices.

1. Place onion, garlic, ginger and spices in 3-quart
   casserole. Cover and cook at 100% power (high)
   for 3 to 4 minutes.

2. Add chicken, recover and cook at 100% power
   (high) for 15 to 20 minutes or until chicken
   reaches a temperature of 170 degrees.

3. Stir in tomatoes and yogurt. Recover and cook
   at 100% power (high) for 10 minutes.

4. Sprinkle with garam marsala, lemon juice and
   corriander to serve.

▼ ▼ ▼

Brandied Chicken Breasts

TO SERVE 4

4 chicken breasts,
  skinned
¼ cup brandy
1 teaspoon dried thyme
1 tablespoon paprika
2 tablespoons butter
2 tablespoons flour
1 cup lowfat buttermilk

Don't worry about all the brandy in this recipe. The alcohol cooks off imparting a delicious taste to the chicken.

1. Place chicken, brandy, thyme and paprika in a 2-quart ring pan. Cover and cook at 100% power (high) for 8 to 10 minutes. Set aside.
2. Place butter and flour in a 2-cup bowl. Cook at 100% power (high) 2 minutes, stirring occasionally to make a roux.
3. Stir in buttermilk and the juices from the chicken. Cook at 100% power (high) for 3 to 5 minutes, stirring every 30 seconds until thick and smooth.
4. Pour over chicken and serve.

▼ ▼ ▼

Spicy, Cheesy Chicken Breasts

TO SERVE 4

4 chicken breasts, boned
¾ cup dry white wine
1 tablespoon cajun spice
  mix, or blend
  1/2 teaspoon cayenne
  pepper, 1/4 teaspoon
  dry mustard, 1/4
  teaspoon white pepper
  and 2 teaspoons fine
  herbs
1 cup shredded Swiss
  cheese
2 tablespoons
  cornstarch
1 cup plain yogurt

With their delicate flavor and fine texture, chicken breasts lend themselves to a wide variety of uses. Cajun-style spices and good Swiss cheese, with a little tang, are a fine combination.

1. Place chicken breasts, wine and herbs in 1-quart casserole. Cover and cook at 70% power (medium-high) for 8 to 10 minutes, or to a temperature of 160 degrees.
2. Coat cheese with cornstarch and mix with yogurt.
3. Drain chicken juice into cheese mixture. Stir and cook at 100% power (high) for 3 to 4 minutes or until cheese has melted and mixture is smooth.
4. Pour over breasts.

▾ ▾ ▾   # Chicken Cacciatora

TO SERVE 4

1 medium onion,
  chopped
1 bell pepper, seeded and
  chopped
4 cloves garlic, chopped
1 pound mushrooms,
  sliced
1 pound Italian sausage,
  skin removed and cut
  into 1-inch pieces
1 frying chicken
  (3 to 4 lbs.), skinned
  and cut up
2 bay leaves
2 tablespoons dried
  Italian herbs
1 teaspoon dried chilli
  peppers
1 can (25 oz.) crushed
  tomatoes
1 cup dry red wine

There are many versions of this "Hunter's Style" chicken and I know you'll like this one. But be creative and add your personal touch to the recipe. This is a good way to demonstrate that microwave cooking is as good as doing it conventionally. Use frozen vegetables where appropriate.

1. Crack the large bones of the chicken with a heavy knife or cleaver.
2. Place the onion, bell pepper, garlic, mushrooms and sausage in 3-quart casserole. Cook at 100% power (high), covered, for 5 minutes.
3. Add the chicken, herbs and chili pepper. Recover and cook at 100% power (high) for 15 to 20 minutes, rearranging chicken once for even cooking.
4. Stir in tomatoes and wine and cook at 100% power (high) for 10 minutes.

▼ ▼ ▼

Chicken Potenza

TO SERVE 4

2 large baking potatoes

1 chicken, cut up
and skinned
(2 to 2½ lbs.)

1 large onion, sliced

½ teaspoon red pepper
flakes

1 cup dry white wine

2 large ripe tomatoes,
chopped or 1 14-oz.
can sliced tomatoes,
drained

¼ cup chopped fresh
parsley

12 leaves fresh basil,
chopped

Olive oil (to coat
pototoes)

Italian recipes have always been my favorites, so I was
particularly pleased when San Francisco restauranteur
Carlo Middione agreed to be a guest on my television
show. His book, "The Food of Southern Italy,"
(William Morrow and Company) is wonderful, and
some of the recipes can be converted to microwave
cooking.

1. Cut potatoes lengthwise into ½-inch slices.
   Place slices on a 9"x 13" roasting rack and cook at
   100% power (high), uncovered, for 10 minutes.
   Set aside.

2. Place chicken, onion, red pepper flakes, wine,
   tomatoes, parsley and basil in a 2-quart ring pan.
   Cover and cook at 100% power (high) for 20
   minutes.

3. In the meantime, rub olive oil over potatoes and
   bake in conventional oven at 400 degrees until
   well browned, turning once.

4. Place chicken on serving platter with potatoes.
   Cook sauce from chicken at 100% power (high),
   uncovered, for 5 minutes, or until thickened.
   Pour over chicken and serve.

Original recipe appears in Carlo Middione's *The Food of Southern Italy,* published by William
Morrow and Company, Inc., 1988.

Chicken Florentine

1 bag (16 oz.) frozen
  chopped spinach
1 cup mushrooms,
  minced
1 small onion, minced
2 tablespoons butter
2 tablespoons good
  quality mustard
1 fryer (3 lbs.), cut-up,
  or 4 chicken breasts,
  skinned

When you see the word "Florentine" in a recipe, it means it originated in Florence, Italy and will always include spinach as an ingredient.

1. Cook spinach at 100% power (high) in a 3-quart casserole dish as instructed on package. Squeeze out water.
2. Place mushrooms, onion and butter in 1½-quart cook-and-measure bowl. Cook at 100% power (high), uncovered for 4 to 5 minutes. Stir in mustard.
3. Place chicken on spinach, cover and cook at 100% power (high) high for 18 to 20 minutes or to a temperature of 170 degrees.
4. Reheat sauce and spoon over chicken to serve.

Barbeque Chicken

1 frying chicken, cut
  up and skinned
  (3 to 4 lbs.)

Marinade

½ cup apple vinegar
¼ cup oil
1 tablespoon
  Worchestershire sauce
1 tablespoon dried
  onion flakes
1 tablespoon Tabasco
  sauce
½ teaspoon dry mustard
2 tablespoons paprika

You can serve this cooked only by microwave, or do it in combination with your charcoal grill for additional flavor and color.

1. Mix marinade ingredients and pour over chicken in a 2-quart ring pan. Marinate for an hour or so.
2. Cover and cook at 100% power (high) for 15 minutes. Turn pieces over once.
3. It is now ready for grilling. Use the marinade for basting. If you don't want to grill it, cook at 100% power (high) for 5 minutes more or to a temperature of 170 degrees, and it's ready to serve.
4. Reduce the marinade by cooking 10 minutes at 100% power (high). Pour over chicken to serve.

▼ ▼ ▼

Pickled Chicken or Turkey

TO SERVE 4

1 cup kosher salt

1 cup sugar

½ cup vinegar

2 yellow onions, stuck with cloves

1 tablespoon ground mace

1 tablespoon peppercorns, smashed

2 bay leaves (or use 1/2 cup pickling spice to replace the mace, bays leaves and peppercorns)

1 small turkey or large roaster (7 to 10 lbs.), skin removed

Pickling poultry may sound a little unusual. But trust me and try it. The flavors blend beautifully.

1. Mix salt, sugar, vinegar and spices. Cook at 100% power (high) until salt and sugar dissolve, about 4 to 5 minutes.
2. Insert onions in cavity of bird. Place bird in 3-quart, high-sided casserole dish. Add pickling juice, cover and marinate overnight.
3. Cook at 100% power (high) 10 minutes per pound, turning bird over once.
4. Remove from the brine and serve hot or cold with horseradish sauce.

▼ ▼ ▼

Taco Turkey Wings

TO SERVE 2

2 turkey wings (or thighs) about 2½ lbs.

2 cups water

1 can (10 oz.) stewed tomatoes

1 package (1¼ oz.) taco seasoning mix

1 cup shredded cheddar cheese

Sometimes turkey parts are featured at your local market at really low prices. That's the time to make this recipe.

1. Place turkey parts in a 3-quart rectangular dish and add water.
2. Crimp the edges of a piece of aluminum foil big enough to cover the area of the turkey and place it right on top of the turkey.
3. Cover the dish with plastic wrap and cook at 100% power (high) for 10 minutes.
4. Reduce power to 50% (medium) and cook for an additional 20 minutes. Drain off juices.
4. Combine tomatoes and taco seasoning and pour over turkey. Cook at 100% power (high) for 5 minutes.
5. Top with cheese and cook at 100% power (high) for 1 to 2 minutes until cheese melts.

▾ ▾ ▾   # Cornish Hens

TO SERVE 4

3 tablespoons sesame oil

3 tablespoons garlic
powder

4 cornish hens (1 to 1½
lbs. each)

Using both your microwave and your conventional oven for this recipe, you get an extremely moist bird with a crispy brown skin.

1. Mix together oil and garlic powder and paint each bird with the mixture.
2. Place in a 2-quart ring pan or a 3-quart rectangular dish.
3. Cover and cook at 100% power (high) for 20 to 25 minutes or to a temperature of 160 degrees. Turn birds over and inside to outside after 10 minutes for even cooking.
4. In the meantime, pre-heat your conventional oven to 500 degrees.
5. Transfer the birds to conventional oven and bake for 10 to 15 minutes or until brown.

Microduck Sauté

▼ ▼ ▼

TO SERVE 4

1 duckling (4 to 5 lbs.)

¼ cup chicken stock

2 tablespoons soy sauce

2 tablespoons dry sherry

1 teaspoon sesame oil

2 teaspoons cornstarch

1 medium red bell
pepper, thinly sliced

1 medium green bell
pepper, thinly sliced

1 small carrot, cut into
matchstick-sized
pieces

2 scallions, cut into
2-inch pieces

2 cups bean sprouts

Martin Yan, star of the PBS television series "Yan Can Cook" is truly a cooking showman. When he appears on my show, the time flies; and so do the onions, carrots and celery. He's a veritable Chinese food processor when he has a cleaver in his hand. Here are some samples of his special style of Chinese cooking adapted for the microwave oven.

Martin was a little surprised at how well you can steam a duck in a microwave oven, when he did the recipe on my show. He prepared the rest of the dish in a wok, but I've converted the entire dish for microwave cooking.

1. Place duck in cooker/steamer inside a 3-quart casserole dish. Cover and cook at 100% power (high) for 25 to 30 minutes. Remove duck and allow to cool.
2. Discard skin and strip meat from bones. Set aside.
3. Place chicken stock, soy sauce, sherry, sesame oil, cornstarch, bell peppers, carrots, scallions and bean sprouts in 3-quart casserole. Cover and cook at 100% power (high) for 5 to 6 minutes, or until vegetables are cooked tender-crisp.
4. Add duck, stir and serve.

Note: Duckling also roasts beautifully in a microwave oven. The best way is to microwave it, covered, for about 7 minutes per pound. Then transfer it to a metal pan and roast conventionally in a preheated 500 degree oven for 10 to 15 minutes or until the skin is crisp. Baste while roasting with your favorite duck sauce.

▼

Beef,
Pork
&
Lamb

▼

Brisket Italiano

Hearty Beef Stew

Beef Short Ribs

Swiss Steak Mexican

Good Ol' American
Brisket

Sloppy Joes

Beef Stroganoff

Tamale Pie

Chili

Easy Osso Buco

Koenigsburger Klopse

Veal Stew Elegante

Herbed Roast Veal

Crown Roast of Pork

Braised Pork-Filled
Cucumbers

▼ ▼ ▼

▼

Kielbasa-Stuffed
Pork Loin

Pork Chile / Chili

Pork Barbeque

Country Ham

Sweet & Sour Pork

Dill Lamb Roast

Stuffed Leg of Lamb
with Herb Mustard

Lamb with Couscous

Lamb Gumbo

Lamb Cassoulet

▼ ▼ ▼

BEEF, PORK & LAMB

▼ ▼ ▼

Of all the meats, beef requires the most care when cooked in a microwave oven. All tender roasts—filet, sirloin and rib roasts, for example— should be cooked slowly, at 50 percent power or less. At higher power levels, the outside tends to overcook, while the inside stays raw.

Slow microwave cooking allows the roast to brown, but I still like to use browning enhancers such as MicroShake, soy sauce or Kitchen Bouquet for a little extra color and taste.

As in conventional cooking, tougher cuts of beef—such as pot roast, short ribs and brisket—cook best with the addition of liquid. Cook these cuts at higher power levels, but allow enough time for the meat to tenderize.

If you see an area drying out, cover it aluminum foil to reflect the microwave energy away from that area and prevent overcooking.

Roast veal and stew-type dishes using veal cook beautifully in a microwave oven. Use a lower power setting to be sure the outside doesn't cook too quickly. Veal should be cooked to a temperature of about 160 degrees.

Pork roasts are the easiest meat to cook by microwave. In a microwave oven, the pork doesn't dry out the way it can in conventional cooking. Cook pork roasts beyond rare; to about 160 to 170 degrees.

The secret to perfect pork is to keep the meat tightly covered. This allows the captured steam to help complete the cooking and retains the moisture as well.

Because they are thinner and more of the surface is exposed to the microwave energy, pork chops can overcook and dry out. Therefore, cook them slowly with a liquid or sauce to keep them moist and tender.

Lamb provides a pleasant change from other, more widely-served meats and I make a point of having it at least once a month. Use your microwave oven to prepare larger lamb cuts such as legs and roasts or for stews and curries.

But when it comes to cooking a delicate lamb chop, go back to the conventional cooking; broiling, grilling or pan frying. There just isn't enough mass to have it cook well in a microwave oven.

▾ ▾ ▾

Brisket Italiano

TO SERVE 4

1 beef brisket (2 to 2½ lbs.), trimmed of all exterior fat

2 medium yellow onions, sliced

4 large cloves garlic, smashed

3 tablespoons spaghetti sauce seasoning or Italian herb blend

1 cup beef stock

1 cup dry red wine

1½ cups prepared spaghetti sauce

Brisket is a tough cut of meat, so it requires long cooking to tenderize it. But it's very flavorful and microwave cooking reduces the cooking time substantially.

1. Brown beef in a skillet if you like, though it isn't necessary.
2. Place beef brisket, onions, garlic, spaghetti sauce, beef stock and wine in 3-quart casserole. Cover with foil, then cover dish.
3. Cook at 100% power (high) for 10 minutes. Reduce power to 50% (medium) and cook for an additional 50 minutes. Turn over once.
4. Remove foil and add spaghetti sauce.
5. Recover and cook at 100% power (high) for 10 minutes.

Note: By covering with foil, the microwave cooking energy is reflected away from the meat and to the liquid in the dish. This indirect cooking results in tender brisket.

Hearty Beef Stew

TO SERVE 4

1 medium onion,
  chopped

1 large carrot, chopped

4 cloves garlic, minced

1 tablespoon minced
  parsley

2 bay leaves

1 tablespoon fine herbs

1½ pounds beef stew
  meat

½ cup flour

1 cup dry red wine

1 can (12 oz.) stewed
  tomatoes

2 medium potatoes,
  diced

2 large carrots, sliced

Nothing tastes better on a cold day than good, hot
stew. Try this version and then adapt your favorite
stew recipe to microwave cooking. If you use the ring
pan, you can just set it and forget it. Otherwise stir
once or twice.

1. Place onion, carrot, garlic, parsley, bay leaves
   and herbs in 2-quart ring pan or 3-quart
   casserole dish.

2. Cook, covered, at 100% power (high) for 3 to 4
   minutes.

3. Add beef and flour, stir and cook at 100% power
   (high) for 10 minutes.

4. Stir in wine and tomatoes. Cover and cook at
   100% power (high) for 30 to 40 minutes or until
   beef is tender.

5. Add potatoes and carrots, recover and cook at
   100% power (high) for 10 to 15 minutes.

▼ ▼ ▼

Beef Short Ribs

TO SERVE 4

4 beef short ribs, (about 2½–3 lbs.)

2 cups beef stock

¼ cup brown sugar or molasses

¼ cup liquid hot sauce

3 tablespoons Worchestershire sauce

Beef short ribs are very tough and have to be cooked a long time in order to tenderize them. But their rich flavor is worth the effort.

1. Place ribs in cooker/steamer inside a 3-quart casserole. Cover and cook at 100% power (high) for 15 minutes.
2. Discard fat, remove steamer and place ribs in the 3-quart casserole. Add beef stock, brown sugar or molasses, liquid hot sauce and Worchestershire sauce.
3. Cover and cook at 70% power (medium-high) for 50 minutes. To avoid drying out, either cover the top of the meat with foil or stir them every 15 minutes.

▼ ▼ ▼

Swiss Steak Mexican

TO SERVE 4

2 medium onions, chopped

1 large bell pepper, seeded and chopped

4 cloves garlic, minced

1 round steak (1½ lbs.), cut into 4 pieces

4 tablespoons chili powder

1 can (15 oz.) Mexican-style stewed tomatoes

¼ cup chopped cilantro

Did Swiss steak originate in Switzerland? I don't know. But here's a Latin variation of this well-known dish.

1. Place onions, bell pepper and garlic in ring pan and cook at 100% power (high) for 4 to 5 minutes. Remove.
2. Dust beef with chili powder. Place beef in ring pan and cover with onions and pepper. Pour tomatoes over top.
3. Cover and cook at 50% power (medium) for 30 to 40 minutes or until beef is tender.
4. Sprinkle with cilantro to serve.

Good Ol' American Brisket

TO SERVE 4

1 beef brisket (3 lbs.), trimmed of fat and cut into two equal pieces.

1 can (16 oz.) beef stock

1 package onion soup mix

2 tablespoons cornstarch, diluted with 2 tablespoons water

Using your microwave oven, you can prepare tender brisket in about half the time of conventional cooking with the same delicious results.

1. Place meat in a 3-quart casserole and cook, covered, at 100% power (high) for 10 minutes, turning the meat over and inside to outside for even cooking.

2. Add stock and soup mix. Cover and cook at 70% power (medium high) for 30 minutes. Turn meat again, recover and cook for an additional 30 minutes at 70% power (medium-high).

3. If you see any portion of the meat drying out, place foil on top of all the meat. Test for tenderness. Cook longer if necessary.

4. Remove meat and thicken juices with diluted cornstarch for a delicious gravy.

Sloppy Joes

TO SERVE 4

1 pound lean ground beef

1 can (28 oz.) crushed tomatoes

3 tablespoons brown sugar

1 tablespoon vinegar

1 tablespoon chili powder

Making Sloppy Joes is a good way to introduce children to microwave cooking because it's simple and a dish all kids love.

1. Place beef in cooker/steamer in a 3-quart casserole. Cover, and cook at 100% power (high) for 5 minutes.

2. Discard fat and place beef, tomatoes, brown sugar, vinegar and chili powder back in the 3-quart casserole.

3. Cook at 100% power (high), covered with wax paper, for 15 to 20 minutes, or until thickened.

4. Add 2 tablespoons flour dissolved in 2 tablespoons water if you want a thicker consistency.

5. Serve on hamburger buns or poured over baked potatoes.

▼ ▼ ▼

Beef Stroganoff

1 pound lean ground
beef

2 cups sliced
mushrooms

1 cup chopped onions

2 tablespoons butter

2 tablespoons
Worchestershire sauce

1 can (10½ oz.)
condensed cream of
mushroom soup

1 tablespoon dried dill
weed

Salt and pepper to
taste

½ pint sour cream
Hot cooked noodles

The Russian count Sergei Stroganoff was a fan of beef
cooked with sour cream and mushrooms. He left us
a wonderful legacy in the form of this rich, creamy
dish. Some health-conscious people grimace when
they see the ingredients. But it didn't seem to bother
the count. When he died in 1882, he was 88 years old.

1. Cook beef, covered, in a cooker-steamer at 100%
    power (high) for 5 minutes. Discard fat.
2. Place mushrooms, onions, butter and Worchester-
    shire sauce in the 3-quart casserole. Cook, cov-
    ered, at 100% power (high) for high 5 minutes.
3. Add beef, soup, dill weed, salt and pepper
    to taste.
4. Cook, covered, at 100% power (high) for
    4 minutes.
5. Add sour cream, stirring to blend.
6. Serve over noodles.

▾ ▾ ▾

Tamale Pie

½ cup corn meal

2 cups water

1 tablespoon chili
powder

1 pound lean ground
beef

2 cups cooked chicken,
cut up

1 package (10 oz.) frozen
corn

½ cup frozen chopped
peppers

1 can (14 oz.) Rotel
tomatoes and chillis,
drained

1 cup shredded cheddar
cheese

Traditional Mexican tamales are steamed in corn husks with lard. This recipe eliminates the lard but maintains the flavor. In pie form, it's also much easier to make than the individual tamales.

1. Cook corn meal, water and chili powder, uncovered, in a cook-and-measure bowl for 7 to 8 minutes to make a thick mush for the crust.

2. Line bottom and sides of a 9-inch pie plate with mush about ¼-inch thick.

3. Place ground beef in cooker/steamer set in a 3-quart casserole. Cook, covered, at 100% power (high) for 5 minutes. Pour off fat.

4. Mix together beef, chicken, corn, peppers and tomatoes. Pour into pie shell and top with 1 cup shredded cheddar cheese.

5. Cook, uncovered, at 100% power (high) for 7 to 10 minutes, until cheese is melted and flavors blended.

▼ ▼ ▼

Chili

TO SERVE 4

1 pound beef chorizo
  sausage
1 pound beef rump
  roast, diced
1 cup chopped onions
1 cup chopped green
  pepper
2 tablespoons chopped
  garlic
1 cup water or beer
2 cans (10 oz. each)
  tomatoes and chilies
6 can (6 oz.) tomato
  paste
2 tablespoons chili
  powder
½ teaspoon ground
  cumin
1 teaspoon dried
  oregano
2 cans (15 oz. each) chili,
  pinto, red kidney or
  any other bean of your
  choice, drained

In those chili "cook-offs" that are held around the country, everyone has their own secret recipe. Well, this is my personal microwave favorite. And I'll put it up against any of those prize-winning, all-day-in-the-pot versions. Try them both and decide which you like best.

1. Cook sausage in a ring pan for 5 minutes on 100% power (high). Discard fat.
2. Add beef, onions, pepper and garlic. Cover and cook at 100% power (high) for 8 minutes.
3. Blend in water (or beer), tomatoes and chilies, tomato paste and spices.
4. Cover, cook at 100% power (high) for 10 minutes, then on at 50% power (medium) for about 50 minutes or until beef is very tender. Check thickness and dilute with water, if necessary.
5. Add beans and cook at 100% power (high) for 5 minutes, covered, to heat through.

▾ ▾ ▾

Easy Osso Buco

TO SERVE 4

Gremolata

1 clove garlic, minced

½ cup minced parsley

¼ cup minced lemon
    peel

1 medium onion,
    chopped (or 1/2 cup
    frozen chopped onion)

1 medium carrot, finely
    chopped

2 pounds veal shank,
    cut into 2-inch rounds

1 can (15 oz.) Italian-
    style tomatoes

1 cup dry red wine

1 package oxtail soup
    mix

Another elegant, but easy dish. In one of my previous books, I included a fairly complicated recipe for Osso Buco. But it was quite a chore to demonstrate on my road tours, so I streamlined the recipe and here it is. To be honest, this simple dish actually tastes better than the first one.

1. Combine gremolata ingredients and set aside.
2. In a 2-quart ring pan or 3-quart casserole, cook the the onion and carrot, covered, at 100% power (high) for about 3 minutes.
3. Add the shanks and cook at 100% power (high), covered, for 10 minutes.
4. Mix tomatoes, wine and soup mix and add to shanks. Cover and cook at 100% power (high) for 20 to 25 minutes, or until very tender.
5. Serve shanks with a generous sprinkling of gremolata.

▼ ▼ ▼

Koenigsburger Klopse

TO SERVE 4

½ cup chopped onions

1 tablespoon butter

½ pound each ground beef, pork and veal or turkey

2 eggs

3 tablespoons green peppercorns (or capers), chopped

2 tablespoons anchovy paste

3 tablespoons chopped parsley

½ teaspoon grated lemon peel

2 slices white bread, soaked in milk and squeezed

Gravy

1 cup cream

1 tablespoon butter

1 tablespoon flour

3 tablespoons lemon juice

1 pint sour cream or plain yogurt

You could just call these "German meatballs." But for these—the royalty of meatballs—I like the international sound of their traditional name, "Koenigsburger Klopse", better.

1. Cook onions and butter, uncovered, at 100% power (high) for about 2 minutes.

2. Mix together sauteed onions and other meatball ingredients. Form into 4 equal balls. Place in cooker/steamer in 3-quart casserole, cover, and cook at 100% power (high) for 4 minutes. Turn inside out and recover. Cook at 100% power (high) and additional 4 minutes or to temperature of 160 degrees.

3. Pour off fat and reserve juices. Set meatballs aside.

4. For gravy, cook butter and flour at 100% power (high) for 1 minute.

5. Stir in cream and juices. Cook at 100% power (high) for 2 minutes, or until thick.

6. Add lemon juice and sour cream or yogurt. Mix and pour over meatballs.

7. Serve with noodles, rice or grits.

▾ ▾ ▾ ## Veal Stew Elegante

TO SERVE 4

2 pounds veal stew meat
4 tablespoons butter
1 cup mushrooms, quartered
1 cup chicken stock
4 tablespoons flour
1 package frozen artichoke bottoms, quartered
1 cup pitted ripe olives
1 small can pimentos, drained
¼ cup chopped fresh parsley
Freshly ground pepper

This recipe elevates a simple stew to regal status. Sometimes veal stew meat can be purchased at bargain prices. That's the time to make more than you need and freeze portions for later use.

1. In a 2-quart ring pan, place the veal, butter, mushrooms, chicken stock and flour.
2. Cover and cook at 100% power (high) for 10 minutes. Then reduce power to 50% (medium) for 20 to 30 minutes, or until tender.
3. Add artichoke bottoms, olives and pimentos. Cook at 100% power (high) for 10 minutes.
4. Garnish with parsley and freshly ground pepper.

▾ ▾ ▾ ## Herbed Roast Veal

TO SERVE 4

1 medium onion, chopped
1 large stalk celery, chopped
1 large carrot, chopped
2 cloves garlic, chopped
1 cup dry white wine
2 tablespoons fine herbs
1 teaspoon tarragon
1 boneless veal roast (about 2 lbs.), tied
1 cup cream (or condensed milk)
2 tablespoons cornstarch, diluted with 3 tablespoons water

I'm a strong believer that veal, like lamb, should be served more often. It provides variety to our diets and can be prepared so many interesting ways. Leftovers from this roast make great sandwiches. As a variation, you can substitute turkey for the veal.

1. Place onion, celery, carrot and garlic in 3-quart casserole and cook at 100% power (high), covered, for 4 to 5 minutes or until soft.
2. Add wine, fine herbs, tarragon, veal and cream or condensed milk. Cover and cook at 50% power (medium) for 25 to 30 minutes.
3. Remove roast and set aside. Keep warm.
4. Whisk together cream and cornstarch mixture. Add to pan juices. Stir and cook at 100% power (high) for 2 to 3 minutes, or until just thickened.

▼ ▼ ▼

Crown Roast of Pork

TO SERVE 6 TO 8

1 package (16 oz.)
  stuffing mix
1 crown roast of pork
  (7 to 8 lbs.)
  Salt and pepper to taste

Crown roasts make dramatic presentations for special occasions. Merle Ellis, the butcher, uses stuffing mix when he cooks a pork crown. By covering the bones with aluminum during half of the cooking time, you prevent them from drying out and charring.

1. Prepare stuffing mix as directed on the package.
2. Place the roast on a microwave roasting rack. Spoon the stuffing in the opening in the center of the roast. Season the meat with salt and pepper.
3. Cover the entire roast with plastic wrap. Place a cap of aluminum foil over the bones.
4. Cook at 70% power (medium-high) for 7 to 8 minutes per pound, or to a temperature of 160 degrees. Remove foil half-way through the cooking.
5. Let stand 10 minutes before serving.

Braised Pork-Filled Cucumbers

Martin Yan didn't believe I could make this dish in a microwave oven until I proved it to him on my show. In addition to being easy to do, the color of the cucumber cooked by microwave is actually more vivid than when steamed traditionally.

TO SERVE 4

2 cucumbers, peeled or not

Filling

½ pound lean ground pork
1 tablespoon soy sauce
2 teaspoons sesame oil
1 teaspoon sugar
1 teaspoon cornstarch

Sauce *

½ cup chicken stock
2 tablespoons soy sauce
2 tablespoons dry sherry
1 teaspoon sugar
1 teaspoon cornstarch

1. Remove 1/2 inch from the end of each cucumber. Cut cucumbers into 6 equal round pieces, for a total of 12 cucumber rounds. Scoop out seeds and soft pulp with a melon baller.
2. Mix together filling ingredients and fill each cucumber round.
3. Mix together sauce ingredients. Place 6 filled cucumber rounds in muffin pan and pour 1 tablespoon of sauce over each cucumber.
4. Cover with ring pan or plastic wrap and cook at 100% power (high) for 4 to 5 minutes.
5. Remove to serving platter. Repeat the process for the remaining 6 cucumber rounds.

Original recipe appears in Martin Yan's *The Chinese Chef*, published by Doubleday and Company, Inc., 1985.

▼ ▼ ▼

Kielbasa-Stuffed Pork Loin

TO SERVE 4

1 pork loin (about 2 lbs.)
1 kielbasa or other
   sausage (about 6 in.)

I'm from the Midwest, where sausage is widely served. I also happen to like pork roast cooked by microwave because it stays so moist and tender. Put sausage and pork together and you have something unique and special.

1. With a long, thin knife, make an "x" about 1 inch across into the center and through the entire length of the loin.
2. Insert sausage into the incision. Cut off any sausage that protrudes.
3. Place in a cooker/streamer inserted into a 3-quart casserole. Cover and cook at 100% power (high) for 7 minutes per pound or until the meat reaches 160 degrees.

▼ ▼ ▼

Pork Chile

TO SERVE 4

  2 medium onions,
     chopped
  4 cloves garlic,
     chopped
½ teaspoon cumin
½ teaspoon turmeric
½ teaspoon ground
     oregano
  2 tablespoons flour
1½ pounds boneless
     pork, trimmed and
     cut into 1-inch cubes
  1 cup chicken stock or
     canned broth
  1 can (24 oz.) mashed
     tomatoes
  2 cans (4 oz. each)
     diced green chilies

Most people associate beef with chili. Pork makes a very good chili as well and I like to serve this version for variety.

1. Place onions, garlic, cumin, turmeric and oregano in a 2-quart ring pan. Cover and cook at 100% power (high) for 4 to 5 minutes, or until the onions are soft.
2. Coat pork with flour and add to onions. Cook at 100% power (high), uncovered or covered with wax paper to prevent spattering, for 10 minutes.
3. Add chicken stock or broth, tomatoes and chilies. Cover and cook at 100% power (high) for 25 to 30 minutes or until pork is very tender.

Pork Barbeque

TO SERVE 4

1 pork loin (3 to 4 lbs.), bone in
1 cup water
  Prepared barbeque sauce

Pork just naturally lends itself to being barbequed and it's so easy in a microwave oven. Use this recipe for sandwiches or as a main course.

1. Trim pork of excess fat. Place water in 3-quart casserole dish. Place pork in cooker/steamer and insert into casserole.
2. Cover and cook at 100% power for 40 to 50 minutes. Turn over once during cooking and check for tenderness. There will be some browning and drying, but this is desirable when mixed with the rest of the pork, which will be moist and shred easily with a fork.
3. With two forks, scrape all the meat from the bone and mix with just enough barbeque sauce to coat the meat.
4. Cook at 100% power, covered, for another 10 minutes.

▼ ▼ ▼

Country Ham

TO SERVE 4

1 country ham (about 7 lbs.), cured (not cooked), with bone in

1 package (16 oz.) frozen, chopped collard greens, thawed

In the south, ham and fresh collard greens are a popular and complementary combination. Fresh collard greens aren't found as commonly in other parts of the country, but you can get frozen collard almost anywhere and it's delicious.

Serves 4, with ham left over for pea soup or a casserole.

1. Trim all surface fat, leaving about 6 pounds of ham.
2. Place in 3-quart 9" x 13" rectangular pan. Add 3 cups water, cover with plastic wrap and cook at 100% power (high) for 20 minutes.
3. Turn over and taste water. If very salty, replace with fresh water. Cover and cook at 100% power (high) for additional 20 minutes.
4. Place chopped collard greens around the ham. Cover and cook at 100% power (high) for another 40 minutes or until ham reaches a temperature of 160 degrees.

Bacon, Cooking

If there's one thing that gets people excited about using their microwave oven, it's cooking bacon. It's quicker and there's much less mess. In addition, you reduce the amount of fat because the meat doesn't lie in it while it cooks. Using a microwave cooking rack, the fat drains off, which is much healthier for you. It's actually like broiling the bacon.

The cooking time depends on the temperature of the bacon when you begin cooking and the thickness.

Place the bacon—slices separated—on a cooking rack with a paper towel on top to avoid spattering. If you don't have a rack, a plate or platter will do, but put one or two pieces of paper towel on the bottom to absorb the fat.

For regular bacon, plan on 1 minute per slice if you begin at room temperature. Right out of the refrigerator, the cooking time will be as much as 1 minute 30 seconds per slice.

If you're cooking thin-sliced bacon, reduce the cooking time to about 45 seconds per slice and watch it so it doesn't overcook.

Thick-sliced bacon should be cooked at medium (50%) power for 2–3 minutes per slice. The slower cooking allows the bacon to brown. But once again, check during the cooking process to be sure you don't overcook.

Also, remember when you're cooking several slices, be prepared to reduce the total time somewhat. For example, with 4 slices, don't set it at 4 minutes and leave it. Take a look at 3 minutes 30 seconds and see how it's doing.

▼ ▼ ▼

Sweet & Sour Pork

TO SERVE 4

1½ pounds lean, boneless pork, cut into thin slices

1 medium onion, cut into large pieces

1 medium green pepper, cored and cut into 1-inch squares

1 medium carrot, cut into ¼-inch slices

1 can (20 oz.) pineapple chunks, with juice

2 tablespoons molasses

2 tablespoons brown sugar

½ cup vinegar

3 tablespoons cornstarch, mixed with 3 tablespoons water

When you try this Cantonese classic in your microwave, you'll send your wok for a walk.

1. Place pork, onion, pepper and carrot in 2-quart ring pan. Cover and cook at 100% power (high) for 10 minutes.
2. Add pineapple, molasses, brown sugar and vinegar. Recover and cook at 70% power (medium high) for 10 minutes.
3. Stir in cornstarch mixture. Cook at 70% power (medium high) for 2 to 3 minutes or until juices thicken.
4. Serve over hot cooked rice.

Dill Lamb Roast

▼ ▼ ▼

TO SERVE 4

1 piece of leg of lamb (about 2 lbs.), boned and tied

½ cup oil

2 tablespoons melted butter

¼ cup lemon juice

4 cloves garlic, minced

1 teaspoon garlic powder

2 tablespoons dried dill weed

1 tablespoon MicroShake browning agent

If you like dill as I do, you'll love this roast. It's a little different than the standard rosemary seasoning usually used when cooking lamb. It also demonstrates how well you can do a roast in a microwave oven.

1. Pierce the roast with a french knife 4 times on each side.
2. Mix the oil, butter, lemon juice, garlic, dill weed and browning agent and pour over the meat, forcing part of the liquid into the holes.
3. Place on a roasting rack and cover with wax paper. Cook at 70% power (medium high) for 8 minutes.
4. Turn meat over, baste with juices, and cook at 70% power (medium high) for an additional 5 to 7 minutes, or to a temperature of 140 degrees.

Stuffed Leg of Lamb with Herb Mustard

▾ ▾ ▾

TO SERVE 4

1 leg of lamb (about 3 lbs.), boned and butterflied

1 jar (4 oz.) marinated artichoke hearts

2 cloves garlic, mashed

2 tablespoons dry vermouth

2 tablespoons Dijon mustard

1 teaspoon Coleman's mustard powder

2 tablespoons dried Italian herbs

2 tablespoons MicroShake browning powder

Because of his wealth of practical information regarding meat buying, cutting and I cooking, I try to have Merle Ellis on my show as often as possible. His newspaper column, "The Butcher," is nationally syndicated. And his book "Cutting Up in the Kitchen" should be required reading for anyone who has ever applied heat to meat. Here's proof that Merle cooks meat as well as he cuts it.

1. Open lamb and spread out flat. Arrange artichokes and artichoke marinade over the lamb.
2. Tie into a roast with butcher's twine.
3. Mix together and blend garlic, vermouth, mustard, mustard powder, herbs and browning powder into a sauce.
4. Coat meat with the sauce.
5. Place in a cooker/steamer in a 3-quart casserole and cook, uncovered, at 70% power (medium high) for 7 minutes per pound, or until the lamb reaches a temperature of 140 degrees.
6. Place in a microwave roasting pan

▼ ▼ ▼

Lamb with Couscous

TO SERVE 4

1 large onion, chopped
4 cloves garlic, minced
4 tablespoons butter
1½ pounds lean lamb stew meat
1 cinnamon stick
1 cup chicken stock
1 apple, chopped
1 orange, skinned and chopped
1 cup couscous

Lamb cooked with locally grown grains is a staple item on tables in the Middle Eastern. With lots of fiber and the wonderful flavor of lamb, it's an appealing addition to our menus as well. Supermarkets generally carry it, though you may have to look in the specialty foods section. For additional flavor, add 1/2 cup orange marmalade, fig preserves or mango chutney.

1. In a 3-quart casserole, cook onion, garlic and butter, covered, at 100% power (high) for 3 to 4 minutes.
2. Add lamb and cinnamon. Cook at 100% power (high), covered, for 10 minutes.
3. Add chicken stock, apple, orange and couscous. Cover and cook at 100% power (high) for 10 minutes, or until couscous is soft.

▼ ▼ ▼

Lamb Gumbo

TO SERVE 4

½ cup flour
½ cup oil
1 medium onion, chopped
1 stalk celery, chopped
1 bell pepper, seeded and chopped
2 pounds lamb stew meat
1 can (15 oz.) stewed tomatoes
1 cup water
1 package (10 oz.) frozen okra
Hot sauce to taste

Lamb stew meat is usually a very good bargain and perfect for this hearty dish with a cajun twist.

1. Place oil and flour in 1-quart heat-proof glass bowl. Cook at 100% power (high) for 7 to 8 minutes, stirring often, until flour becomes brown and has a nutty aroma.
2. Add onion, celery and pepper. Cook at 100% power (high) for 3 to 4 minutes, until soft.
3. Place in 3-quart casserole and add lamb, tomatoes, water, okra and hot sauce.
4. Cook, covered, at 70% power (medium high) for 15 to 20 minutes or until lamb is tender. Add more water if the stew gets too thick. Serve with cooked rice.

▼ ▼ ▼

**Spinach Timbale
with Fresh Tomato Sauce**

Pasta Primavera

**Chicken Potenza
with Grilled Polenta**

▼ ▼ ▼

**Fresh Fruit
in Macadamia Nut Tulip**

▼ ▼ ▼

Lamb Cassoulet

TO SERVE 4

1 lamb breast (about
  2 lbs.)
  MicroShake browning
  agent
1 medium onion,
  chopped
1 medium carrot,
  chopped or sliced
4 cloves garlic, smashed
2 ripe tomatoes, diced or
  1 can (15 oz.) tomatoes,
  drained
2 cans (15 oz. each) white
  beans

This hearty bean casserole is as common in France as pork and beans are here. It's inexpensive, easy to make and tasty.

1. Cut lamb breast into individual ribs. Coat with MicroShake, if desired.

2. Place lamb in cooker/steamer inside a 3-quart casserole dish. Cover and cook at 100% power (high) for 10 to 12 minutes. Discard fat and set aside ribs.

3. Add onions, carrots and garlic to the casserole dish. Cover and cook at 100% power (high) for 4 minutes.

4. Add ribs, tomatoes and beans. Recover and cook at 100% power (high) about 10 minutes to heat thoroughly.

Vegetables

▼

Steamed Artichokes

Asparagus

Asparagus Gratin

Brussels Sprouts

Snap Beans

Green Beans
Vinaigrette

Black Beans Yucateca

Beets

Harvard Beets

Sicilian Broccoli

Broccoli in Orange &
Wine Sauce

Butter-braised Cabbage

Cabbage Rolls Stuffed
with Vegetables

Braised Red Cabbage

Carrots

▼ ▼ ▼

▼

Cauliflower

Braised Belgian Endive

Eggplant, Tomato,
& Fennel

Spicy Eggplant
& Tomatoes

Leeks, Braised
& Lemoned

Swiss-Style Chard

Corn Pudding with
Cheese & Peppers

Okra Succotash

Onions

Peas with Mint
& Scallions

Potato Chips

Mashed Potatoes

Scalloped Potato
Casserole

Stuffed Sweet Potatoes

▼ ▼ ▼

▼

Spicy Vegetables
& Lentils

Etoufee Vegetarian

Wilted Sweet-Sour
Greens

Hollandaise Sauce

Cheese Sauce

Vegetable Butters

▼ ▼ ▼

V E G E T A B L E S

▼ ▼ ▼

Because vegetables have high water content, they're ideally suited to microwave cooking. Use almost no water when microwaving. The moisture from washing fresh vegetables is usually sufficient.

Raw vegetables are best when they're fresh, bright and crisp. In many cases, frozen vegetables are preferable to raw because they're picked at the peak of their flavor. Since they're slightly cooked before freezing, all you have to do is complete the cooking before serving. Also remember that frozen vegetables are cleaned and trimmed, so there's no waste and virtually no preparation time.

When cooking vegetables in your microwave oven be careful not to overcook. Remember the vegetables will continue to cook for a time after the microwave oven is turned off. So slightly undercook them and they'll be right.

▾ ▾ ▾ ## Steamed Artichokes

**1 to 4 medium-sized
artichokes**

One of the attractions of eating an artichoke is that they're fun to eat. Serve them at parties or as a first course anytime.

Because the meat of the choke is at the bottom of each leaf and in the heart, you should cook them upside down. This serves two purposes. First, they'll cook faster because the meat is not immersed in water. And second, because the leaves are in water they won't shrivel and dry up.

Here's the best way I've found to determine how much water you need for cooking. Cut off the leaves just below the prickers and spread them apart without breaking them. Place them under running water to clean between the leaves. The amount of water that remains between the leaves will be perfect for cooking when you invert the artichoke into the cooking dish.

Since a large artichoke will retain more water than a small one, it always turns out to be just the right amount.

This is the purist's way to prepare an artichoke.

1. Trim off prickers and cut off stem. Spread leaves and place under running water. Leave water in the choke and place inverted—top down, that is —into cooking dish. Trim the stems and place them in the dish.
2. Pour 1 tablespoon olive oil on each artichoke and sprinkle with Italian herbs or lemon pepper.
3. Cover, using plastic wrap if the dish has no cover. Cook at 100% power (high) for 7 to 10 minutes per artichoke, or until a knife goes easily into the bottom.
4. Dip the leaves into mayonaise or melted butter or low-cal salad dressing. When all leaves are eaten, remove the thistle, cube the artichoke heart and stem and mix with dressing or dip. That's the best part.
5. Remember to place a large bowl in the center of the table so people can easily dispose of the eaten leaves.

▼ ▼ ▼

Asparagus

TO SERVE 4

1 pound whole asparagas spears

This is a green vegetable I hated as a kid. Now it's my absolute favorite. Maybe I would have liked it better if microwave ovens had been around when I was young, because it's a perfect way to cook asparagas. I love them with hollandaise sauce or vinaigrette sauce.

1. Break off tough ends. Wash and leave the residual water.
2. Place in 1-quart casserole. To insure the tougher stems and more tender tips cook equally, turn half of the spears in the opposite direction.
3. Cover and cook at 100% power (high) for 4 to 6 minutes, depending on how soft you want them.

▼ ▼ ▼

Asparagus Gratin

TO SERVE 4

1 pound cooked asparagas

8 tablespoons butter

1 cup seasoned bread crumbs

½ cup shredded Swiss cheese

¼ cup grated Parmesan cheese

For a very special way to serve asparagas, try them "gratin."

1. Mix together butter and seasoned bread crumbs. Cook at 100% power (high) for 1 minute. Mix and spread over asparagus.
2. Top with Swiss and Parmesan cheeses. Cook at 100% power (high) for 1 minute.

▼ ▼ ▼

Brussels Sprouts

TO SERVE 4

1 pound Brussels sprouts, trimmed

¼ cup butter or olive oil

2 tablespoons lemon juice

Another member of the cabbage family all of which are so good for us. You've never tasted better sprouts than ones cooked by microwave.

1. Place all Brussels sprouts, butter or olive oil and lemon juice in a 1-quart casserole.
2. Cover and cook at 100% power (high) for 6 to 7 minutes. Stir to coat.

▼ ▼ ▼   ## Snap Beans

TO SERVE 4

1 pound snap beans,
  trimmed
  Water to cover

This vegetable, like carrots, has a shape and texture that is less than perfect for microwave cooking. If you're not careful they'll shrivel and get tough. You either must just cover them with water or with foil to protect from overcooking.

1. Place in 1-quart casserole. Cover and cook at 100% power (high) for about 7 minutes, or until tender.
2. Or, place beans in 1-quart casserole with ½ cup of water. Tuck aluminum foil over and around them. Cover and cook at 100% power (high) for 5 to 7 minutes. The foil will reflect the microwave energy away from the beans, heating only the water which turns to steam and cooks the beans.
3. Season with your favorite herb or simply salt and pepper.

▼ ▼ ▼   ## Green Beans Vinaigrette

TO SERVE 4

1 pound pole or string
  beans, trimmed
½ cup dried onion flakes
1 cup water
2 tablespoons olive oil
1 tablespoon wine
  vinegar

The spicy, herby vinaigrette flavors go nicely with all sorts of things, among them fresh beans. The use of foil allows the beans to be steamed rather than cooked directly by the microwave energy. That keeps them moist and tender.

1. Place string beans, onion and water in a 1-quart casserole. Tuck foil over and around beans.
2. Cover and cook at 100% power (high) for 8 to 10 minutes.
3. Drain beans.
4. Mix together olive oil and vinegar and pour over beans.

Black Beans Yucateca

▼ ▼ ▼

TO SERVE 4

Oil

½ cup achiote seeds
1½ cups peanut oil
¼ cup achiote oil
1 large onion, chopped
6 cloves garlic, minced
½ cup cilantro, chopped
2 hot chilli peppers, seeded and chopped
1 bell pepper (red preferred), seeded and diced
1 can (14 oz.) black beans

A wonderfully different and spicy side dish, this Mexican treat is also a good source of fiber. The achiote oil that adds the unique color and aroma to many Mexican dishes is simple to make and will last indefinitely in a sealed container stored in the refrigerator. It also stains, so it's advisable to wear an apron when using it.

1. Place seeds and oil in a glass, heat-proof bowl and stir. Cover with waxed paper and cook at 100% power (high) for 6 to 8 minutes, or until you smell the aroma.
2. Combine 1/4 cup of the oil, onion, garlic, cilantro, chilli peppers and bell pepper in a 1-quart casserole dish.
3. Cover and cook at 100% power (high) for 5 to 6 minutes.
4. Stir in beans. Recover and cook at 100% power (high) for 2 to 3 minutes more or until heated through.

Beets

▼ ▼ ▼

2 pounds beets
1 cup water
Butter

Beets take much less time to cook in a microwave oven than using conventional cooking. And don't forget that beet leaves can be chopped and cooked just like spinach. They taste great!

1. Buy tennis-ball sized beets (or slightly smaller). Cut off the stems and leaves.
2. Place in a 2-quart ring pan with water. Cover and cook at 100% power (high) about 5 minutes per beet. Poke with a knife to tell when they're done.
3. Slip off the skins in cold water. Serve with a little butter.

▾ ▾ ▾   # Harvard Beets

TO SERVE 4

½ cup sugar
¼ cup vinegar
2 teaspoons cornstarch
¼ cup water
4 beets, cooked and
  diced

When beets are cooked, and nice and tender, you can do all sorts of interesting things with them. Here are just a few suggestions.

1. Place sugar, vinegar, cornstarch, and water in a cook-and-measure bowl. Cook at 100% power (high) for 1 to 1½ minutes or until thickened. Add to beets and stir to coat.
2. For gingered beets, add 1 teaspoon ground ginger or 1 tablespoon ginger paste to the Harvard beet sauce. Mix, then add to the beets and stir to coat.
3. For maple-flavored beets, use maple syrup instead of sugar.
4. For special beets, mix 1 cup sour cream and 2 tablespoons prepared horseradish. Add to cooked beets.

▾ ▾ ▾   # Sicilian Broccoli

TO SERVE 4

1 large munch fresh
  broccoli (or a 16-oz.
  package frozen
  broccoli stalks)
¼ cup olive oil
1 large onion, sliced
½ cup dry red wine
12 black olives, pitted
  and sliced (oil cured,
  preferred)
4 anchovy fillets, cup up
1 cup shredded
  provolone cheese
  Salt and pepper to
  taste

Here's another example of the Southern Italian touch Italian chef Carlo Middione uses in his dishes.

1. Place broccoli, olive oil, onion, wine olive and anchovy fillets in a 3-quart casserole.
2. Cover and cook at 100% power (high) for 7 to 8 minutes, stirring once.
3. Uncover, add cheese and cook at 100% power (high) for 1 to 2 minutes, or until cheese has melted.

Original recipe appears in Carlo Middione's *The Food of Southern Italy,* published by William Morrow and Company, Inc., 1988.

▼ ▼ ▼

Broccoli in Orange and Wine Sauce

TO SERVE 4

1 package (16 oz.) frozen broccoli with stems, cut into 1-inch pieces (or 1 lb. raw broccoli, stems peeled and cut into 1-inch pieces)

2 cloves garlic, minced

2 tablespoons olive oil

1 tablespoon butter

2 tablespoons orange peel, grated

½ cup orange juice

½ cup dry white wine

Whenever I want to impress an audience with the beauty of microwave cooking, I prepare a broccoli dish. Whether frozen or raw, the color is so bright people can't help but be impressed. And here's an interesting budget fact. Frozen broccoli costs about half as much as raw broccoli.

1. Cook frozen broccoli in microwave oven as instructed on package. (If using raw broccoli, cook at 100% power (high) in 3-quart casserole, covered, for 5 to 7 minutes.

2. Mix juices with garlic, olive oil, butter, orange peel, orange juice and wine in a cook-and-measure bowl.

3. Cover with a paper towel and cook at 100% power (high) for 8 to 10 minutes or until reduced by one half.

4. Pour over broccoli and toss to coat.

▼ ▼ ▼

Butter-braised Cabbage

TO SERVE 4

½ cabbage (about 1 1/2 pounds), cored and chopped

4 tablespoons butter

Freshly ground pepper

This recipe is so simple and yet so good, you'll make it often.

1. Place cabbage and butter in 3-quart casserole dish. Cook at 100% power (high), covered, for 10 to 12 minutes, or until cabbage is soft. Stir once.

2. Garnish top with freshly ground pepper.

▼ ▼ ▼

Cabbage Rolls Stuffed with Vegetables

TO SERVE 4

4 large cabbage leaves

2 medium red potatoes, diced

¼ pound fresh mushrooms, minced

1 medium apple, cored and diced

½ cup plain yogurt

½ cup chopped almonds

1 cup cooked brown rice

½ cup wheat germ

2 tablespoons curry powder

Cabbage rolls are typically filled with ground meat. But here's a variation to serve for a change or when your vegetarian friends come over.

1. Place whole cabbage leaves in a 1-quart casserole dish. Cover and cook at 100% power (high) for 3 to 4 minutes. Set aside.
2. Cook potatoes, covered, at 100% power (high) for 4 to 6 minutes or until done. Poke to test.
3. Mix all the mushrooms, apple, yogurt, almonds, rice, wheat germ and curry powder together and blend with potatoes.
4. Place an equal amount of mixture on each cabbage leaf.
5. Fold in, roll up and secure with a toothpick.
6. Place in a microwave cooking dish. Cover and cook at 100% power (high) for 7 to 8 minutes.
7. Serve topped with pan juices.

▼ ▼ ▼

Braised Red Cabbage

TO SERVE 4 TO 6

1 pound red cabbage, cored and chopped into large pieces

4 tablespoons butter or olive oil

2 tablespoons brown sugar or molasses

2 apples, cored and sliced

1 medium red onion, chopped

¼ cup lemon juice

½ cup red wine vinegar

Serve it hot or cold. It's especially good with chicken, ham or other pork dishes.

1. Place everything in a 3-quart casserole dish.
2. Cover and cook at 100% power (high) for 12 to 15 minutes, or until soft, stirring once.

▼ ▼ ▼

Carrots

TO SERVE 4

1 pound carrots, left
    whole, cut up or sliced
    lengthwise
Water to cover

I've always loved raw carrots, but for some reason I've never been very fond of cooked ones. However, they taste a little better to me when cooked by microwave, particularly when you add a little something extra.

1. Place in 1-quart casserole or cook-and-measure bowl. Cook at 100% power (high), uncovered, for 8 to 10 minutes, or until tender.
2. Here are a several ways I use to make cooked carrots more interesting. Add 2 to 4 lemon-drop candies or red hots and cook until the carrots are tender. The candy will melt in the process and add a pleasant flavor.
3. Use cola instead of water. Or cover the cooked carrots with a tasty sauce made by combining ½ cup apple juice concentrate and 4 tablespoons butter. Cook at 100% power (high) until blended and then pour over carrots.

▼ ▼ ▼

Cauliflower

TO SERVE 4

1 whole cauliflower
    head
½ cup mayonaise
½ cup shredded Cheddar
    cheese
¼ cup thinly sliced
    scallions
2 tablespoons good
    mustard

An impressive and easy way to microwave cauliflower is to leave the head whole. It'll look beautiful on your table, topped with this simple sauce.

1. Trim off the leaves and wash cauliflower.
2. Place in a 3-quart casserole dish or on a serving platter. Cover with plastic wrap and cook at 100% power (high) for 7 to 8 minutes or until tender.
3. Mix together mayonaise, cheese, scallions and mustard and pour over cauliflower. Cook at 100% power (high), uncovered, about 1 minute, or until cheese is melted.

Braised Belgian Endive

TO SERVE 4

4 Belgian endive heads,
trimmed, halved
lengthwise and cored

3 tablespoons butter or
vegetable oil

Freshly ground pepper
to taste

3 tablespoons fresh
lemon juice

2 tablespoons olive oil
(optional)

3 slices bacon, cooked
and crumbled (or 1/2
cup bacon bits)

Unless you own an endive farm, most of us don't eat this delicate and tasty green. It's just too expensive. But when you want a real treat—a departure from the vegetables you've been eating—try some Belgian endive. Remember, any vegetable braised conventionally can be cooked beautifully by microwave.

1. Place endive, butter and pepper in a 1-quart casserole dish.
2. Cover and cook at 100% power (high) for 10 minutes, or until tender.
3. Splash lemon juice and olive over top and recover until served.
4. Garnish with a sprinkling of crumbled bacon to serve.

Eggplant, Tomato and Fennel

TO SERVE 2 TO 4

4 small Japanese
eggplants, each
pricked 4 times with a
fork

4 large plum tomatoes

½ bulb fennel, cored and
quartered lengthwise

4 large cloves garlic,
smashed and peeled

3 sprigs fresh basil

¼ teaspoon fresh thyme

2 tablespoons olive oil

1 tablespoon water

1 teaspoon kosher salt

Freshly ground black
pepper

When Barbara Kafka made this dish on my show, it particularly pleased the director because it's so photogenic.

1. Arrange eggplants, spoke-fashion, stems toward the center, around the inside rim of a 2-quart soufflé dish. Place tomatoes in center.
2. Scatter fennel on top of eggplant. Tuck garlic, basil and thyme between vegetables.
3. Pour oil, water, salt and pepper over all. Cover tightly with microwave plastic wrap.
4. Cook at 100% power (high) for 15 minutes.
5. Remove from oven. Uncover and let stand for 3 minutes before serving.

Original recipe appears in Barbara Kafka's *Microwave Gourmet,* published by William Morrow and Company, Inc., 1987.

▼ ▼ ▼

Spicy Eggplant & Tomatoes

TO SERVE 4

1 medium onion,
chopped

4 cloves garlic, minced

1 medium bell pepper,
seeded and diced

1 Jalepeno pepper,
seeded and chopped

1 medium eggplant, cut
into large dice, with
skin left on

1 teaspoon tumeric

½ teaspoon cayenne
pepper

1 can (15 oz.) whole
tomatoes, drained and
chopped

4 tablespoons lemon
juice

¼ cup chopped cilantro

Eggplant is relatively bland, so it takes on the flavor of the things cooked with it. In conventional cooking, it's usually fried so it becomes high in calories from the absorbed oil. In microwave cooking, oil is used only for flavoring. Mix this dish with plain yogurt for variety.

1. In the 2-quart ring pan or 3-quart casserole dish, cook the onion, garlic, and peppers, covered, at 100% power (high) for 4 minutes.
2. Add the eggplant, tumeric, cayenne pepper, tomatoes and lemon juice. Recover and cook at 100% power (high) for 8 to 10 minutes, or until soft.
3. Add lemon juice and sprinkle cilantro over top.

▼ ▼ ▼

Leeks, Braised and Lemoned

TO SERVE 4

1 pound fresh leeks
(about 6)

¼ cup olive oil

Juice of 1/2 lemon

Salt and pepper

You won't believe how well leeks cook in a microwave oven. And lemon has just the right flavor to set off wonderful subtleness of these fine greens.

1. Cut off the green part of the leaves and the root ends of leeks. Cut in half, lengthwise and wash.
2. Place in 1-quart casserole with olive oil. Cook at 100% power (high), covered, for 5 to 7 minutes. Rearrange, turning leeks outside to inside and cook at 100% power (high), covered, an additional 2 to 3 minutes.
3. Season with salt and pepper and squeeze the lemon juice over the leaves.

▾ ▾ ▾   ## Swiss-Style Chard

TO SERVE 4

1½ **pound chard leaves, washed and chopped or 1 package (16 oz.) frozen, chopped chard**

½ **pound mushrooms, sliced**

2 **leeks, white part only, thinly sliced**

1 **large clove garlic, minced**

½ **cup celery, chopped**

½ **cup watercress, chopped (optional)**

2 **slices whole wheat bread**

¼ **cup low-fat milk**

1 **cup low-fat Swiss or Gruyere cheese, shredded**

4 **large eggs (whites only, if reducing fat and cholesterol)**

Freshly ground pepper and nutmeg to taste

This recipe has enough variety of the essential food groups to be served as a nutritious one-dish casserole. It's very tasty, but if you want to jazz it up, top it with some nice, hot picante sauce. Remember to save all juices from cooked vegetables and freeze for use in stocks and soups.

1. Place in chard, mushrooms, leeks, garlic, celery and watercress in 3-quart casserole dish. Cover and cook at 100% power (high) for 5 to 7 minutes or until the vegetables are soft. Press and drain off liquid.

2. Mix together bread, milk, cheese and eggs until well blended. Add to the vegetable mixture, blend and pour into 2-quart ring pan. (Note: The ring pan is the most useful dish available for custard type dishes because the center is void. This allows even cooking without tending or stirring.)

3. Cook at 70% power (medium-high) for 6 to 8 minutes, or until set.

▼ ▼ ▼   Corn Pudding with Cheese & Peppers

TO SERVE 4

1 medium green bell pepper, seeded and chopped

1 small onion, chopped

1 package (10 oz.) frozen corn kernels

3 eggs

2 cups milk

1 cup shredded Swiss cheese

4 tablespoons chopped sun-dried tomatoes

½ teaspoon seasoned salt

At my house, we serve corn pudding as a side dish with Thanksgiving dinner.

1. Place pepper and onion in 1-quart casserole. Cover and cook at 100% power (high) for 4 minutes.
2. Add corn, cover and cook at 100% power (high) for 4 minutes.
3. Mix together eggs, milk, cheese, tomatoes and salt. Pour over corn and peppers. Stir, recover, and cook at 70% power (medium-high) about 10 minutes, or until custard has set.

Corn on the Cob

There's nothing more traditionally American than corn-on-the-cob. And there's no easier way to cook it than in your microwave oven.

Place corn in a 3-quart casserole dish and MW, covered about 2 minutes per ear. But deduct a little time if you're doing more than one. For example, cook two ears 3 minutes, 45 seconds and then check for doneness. You can add butter, salt and pepper to the corn before cooking.

Here are some tips and variations you may want to try.

▼ Put butter, salt and pepper on the raw corn, wrap in plastic wrap and cook.

▼ Insert the metal pronged holders into the ears of corn before you cook it, and you'll avoid having to handle the hot corn after cooking.

▼ Fill a wide-mouth jar or grip-and-measure bowl about ⅔ full of water. MW until warm. Melt ¼ pound butter in a small cup and pour into the water. It will float to the top. Dip corn into the water and when you lift it out slowly, it will be perfectly coated with butter.

▾ ▾ ▾   Okra Succotash

TO SERVE 4

1 medium onion, sliced
4 cloves garlic, minced
1 package (10 oz.)
   frozen okra
1 package (10 oz.)
   frozen corn
4 ripe tomatoes,
   chopped or 1 can
   (15 oz.) stewed
   tomatoes
½ teaspoon white
   pepper
1½ teaspoon cayenne
   pepper
2 bay leaves
1 tablespoon dried
   oregano
1 teaspoon dried basil
1 teaspoon dried thyme
1½ teaspoon white
   vinegar

Brad Borel is a delightful man with a commitment to preparing the best of Louisiana's distinctive cuisine at his Bon Temps restaurant in San Francisco. When he appeared as one of the guest chefs on my show, he did a number of his favorite recipes, which I've converted for microwave cooking. Usually succotash is a combination of corn and lima beans. But Brad makes it in a spicy Louisiana-style using okra instead of beans.

1. Place onions and garlic in 3-quart casserole dish. Cover and cook at 100% power (high) for 3 minutes.
2. Add okra, corn, tomatoes, white pepper, cayenne pepper, bay leaves, oregano, basil an thyme. Recover and cook at 100% power (high) about 20 minutes or until okra is thoroughly cooked and succotash is thick. Stir once during cooking.
3. Add vinegar, stir and serve.

▾ ▾ ▾   Onions

TO SERVE 4

4 large yellow onions,
   peeled and halved
4 tablespoons butter
4 tablespoons brown
   sugar

I use onions primarily as seasoning for other recipes. But sugar-topped onion halves make a super-simple and super-good side dish.

1. Place onions in a 1-quart casserole dish. Top each with butter and sugar.
2. Cover and cook at 100% power (high) for 8 to 10 minutes, or until onions are soft.

▼ ▼ ▼

Peas with Mint and Scallions

TO SERVE 4 TO 6

4 tablespoons unsalted butter

2 packages (10 oz.) frozen tiny peas or 2 cups shelled fresh peas (about 1½ lb. in the pod)

1 bunch scallions, trimmed and cut (or 1 cup frozen pearl onions)

¼ cup fresh mint leaves, shredded (or 1 teaspoon dried mint)

Kosher salt

Freshly ground black pepper

In this recipe, Barbara Kafka proves that delightful gourmet dishes can be simple to prepare. As a variation, she suggests stirring in 1½ cups shredded Boston lettuce before the final cooking. Then cook at 100% power (high), uncovered, for 1 minute. Salt and pepper to taste.

1. Defrost peas in a sieve under warm running water.
2. Heat butter in 1½-quart souffle dish, uncovered, at 100% power (high) for 2 minutes.
3. Stir in peas, scallions and mint. Cover tightly with microwave plastic wrap. Cook at 100% power (high) for 3 minutes.
4. Remove from oven. Uncover and stir in salt and pepper. Serve hot.

Original recipe appears in Barbara Kafka's *Microwave Gourmet*, published by William Morrow and Company, Inc., 1987.

▼ ▼ ▼

Potato Chips

1 large baking potato

As good as they taste, packaged potato chips are loaded with fat and salt. Nutritionists encourage us to reduce our consumption of both and it's easy to make fat-free, salt-free potato chips in your microwave oven. They're unique and different from the commercial kind. But very tasty and a whole lot better for you.

1. You can peel the potato first, but I prefer to leave the skin on. Slice the potato into ¼-inch rounds.
2. Place the slices around the edge of a microwave roasting rack and cook at 100% power (high), uncovered, for about 8 to 10 minutes or until they start to brown.
3. If you're not all that worried about fat and salt, coat the chips with non-stick cooking spray and season with salt.

▾ ▾ ▾

Mashed Potatoes

TO SERVE 4

2 medium Idaho potatoes
1 cup milk or cream
  Butter to taste

We often think of mashed pototoes as a "common" dish that we hesitate to serve except with holiday turkey. The fact is that well-prepared mashed potatoes are a wonderful accompaniment to many types of dishes, including those we label "gourmet". For the best-ever mashed potatoes, add 1/2 cup roasted garlic and mix.

1. Always use the best quality potatoes available. You needn't peel them unless you choose to. Microwave potatoes until done, about 5 minutes each. Mash or process in a food mill or ricer.
2. Add milk and butter. Stir to blend.

Potatoes

Potatoes are one of the easiest vegetables to cook in a microwave oven. Yet I receive more questions and complaints about them than any other vegetable. Here are some suggestions and ideas.

The biggest problem is determining when they are done to avoid overcooking them. This question comes from the lack of uniformity in potato size and the range of quality of potatoes.

The average 8-ounce Russet (Idaho) potato will take about 7 to 8 minutes to cook, though this will vary depending on starting temperature and the power of your oven.

If you have an instant-reading thermometer or probe on your oven, stop cooking at 175 degrees and let the potato sit for a couple of minutes. It should be perfect.

You want a dry crusty skin on your potato? After microwaving, place them in an oven pre-heated to 500 degrees or under the broiler for a couple of minutes.

Incidentally, I've never poked a potato before cooking and none has ever burst on me.

New potatoes or red potatoes always microwave perfectly.

Finally, anytime you find a recipe that calls for boiled potatoes, use your microwave instead. Just add about ½ cup water to provide extra moisture.

▼ ▼ ▼

Scalloped Potato Casserole

2 large Russet potatoes
1 medium onion, sliced
2 slices bacon, chopped
1 can (10 oz.) cream of celery soup
½ cup milk
Salt and pepper to taste
1 cup shredded cheddar cheese

This is a version of the old standard recipe for scalloped potatoes. Done in a microwave oven, it tastes the same, but cooks much faster.

1. Cook the potatoes at 100% power (high), covered, for 10 minutes, then slice them into ¼-inch rounds.
2. In a 2-quart ring pan, layer the potatoes, onions and bacon.
3. Mix soup and milk, then add salt and pepper. Pour over potatoes.
4. Cook at 100% power (high), covered, for 12 minutes. Then add cheese and cook at 100% power (high), covered, for an additional 3 minutes.

▼ ▼ ▼

Stuffed Sweet Potatoes

TO SERVE 1 OR 2

1 medium sweet potato
2 tablespoons butter
1 ounce maple syrup or molasses
¼ cup chopped walnuts or pecans

Here's a way to convert a simple potato into a sweet treat. It's great with ham or turkey.

1. Cook sweet potato at 100% power (high) for about 5 to 7 minutes, or 180 degrees or until done when tested with a knife.
2. Cut in half lengthwise and scoop the cooked potato into a bowl. Mix with butter, maple syrup or molasses and nuts.
3. If the butter doesn't melt from the heat of the potato, cook at 100% power (high) for about 1 minute.
4. Stuff the potato back into the potato skin and serve.

▾ ▾ ▾

Spicy Vegetables & Lentils

TO SERVE 4

½ cup dried lentils

1¾ cup water

1 medium onion, chopped

2 carrots, sliced

1 Anaheim chilli, seeded and chopped or 1/4 teaspoon dried chilli pepper flakes

4 cloves garlic, minced

2 cups broccoli flowerettes

2 cups cauliflower flowerettes

1 medium bell pepper, cored and chopped

2 cups cabbage, chopped

4 tablespoons minced fresh ginger

½ teaspoon each cumin, coriander, tumeric, curry powder

¼ cup lemon juice

½ cup hot salsa

Vegetarian dishes such as this can be served as a complete meal. There's lots of fiber and protein for good nutrition. As with rice, the lentils won't cook any faster by microwave. But because the cooking dish doesn't get hot, you don't have to worry about burning or scorching.

1. Place lentils and water in 1½-quart microwave cook-and-measure bowl. Cook at 100% power (high), uncovered, about 20 minutes or until lentils are tender.

2. In a 3-quart casserole dish, cook the onion, carrots, chilli and garlic at 100% power (high) for 3 to 4 minutes, covered.

3. Add the broccoli, cauliflower, bell pepper, cabbage, ginger, spices, lemon juice and salsa. Recover, and cook at 100% power (high) for 12 to 15 minutes, stirring once.

4. Stir in the lentils and adjust seasonings to taste.

▼ ▼ ▼

Etouffee Vegetarian

TO SERVE 4 OR MORE

½ cup flour
½ cup oil
1 cup chopped celery
1 cup chopped bell pepper
1 cup chopped scallions
1 can (16 oz.) stewed tomatoes
1 can (6 oz.) V-8 juice
¼ to 1/2 cup liquid hot sauce
1 can (15 oz.) garbanzo beans
4 cups raw or frozen vegetables, cooked (broccoli, cauliflower, carrots, beans, mushrooms and potatoes all work well)

The basic roux and sauce for seafood etouffee is such a dandy I thought it might work well with vegetables. Was I ever right! Very tasty, much less expensive than seafood and ideal for serving to your vegetarian friends.

1. In a 4-cup, heat-proof glass measuring cup, cook the the flour and oil, uncovered, at 100% power (high) for 6 to 7 minutes. Stir in 1-minute increments after the roux begins to brown. Be careful not to burn. Remember, the handle will be hot.

2. Add celery, pepper and scallions. Stir and cook at 100% power (high) for 3 minutes.

3. Add tomatoes, V-8 juice, hot sauce and garbanzo beans. Cook at 100% power (high), uncovered, for 5 minutes, or until thickened. Dilute with water if too thick.
    Mix with cooked vegetables to serve.

▼ ▼ ▼

Wilted Sweet-Sour Greens

TO SERVE 4

2 tablespoons vegetable oil
2 tablespoons sugar
¼ cup vinegar
1 package (16 oz.) frozen spinach, collard greens, turnip greens, or any combination of leafy greens (or 6 cups of raw greens, washed and chopped, except collard greens, which require long cooking)
1 cup scallions, chopped

In this case, "wilted" means slightly cooked and delicious, not "droopy".

1. Place oil, sugar and vinegar in 3-quart casserole. Cook at 100% power (high), uncovered, for 1 minute or until sugar dissolves.

2. Add vegetables and stir to coat with liquid. Cover and cook at 100% power (high) for 5 to 7 minutes for raw vegetables, or according to package instructions for frozen vegetables.

▾ ▾ ▾   # Hollandaise Sauce

¼ pound butter
3 egg yolks
⅛ teaspoon dry mustard
2 tablespoons lemon
   juice
4 drops Tabasco sauce
⅛ tablespoon
   Worcestershire sauce

Many people are intimidated by Hollandaise sauce, thinking it's one of those things that you have to master. Not so in a microwave oven. It's very nearly foolproof.

1. Place butter in cook-and-measure bowl and cook at 100% power (high) for 10 to 15 seconds to soften.
2. Mix together egg yolks and lemon juice and add to the butter.
3. Cook at 100% power (high) for approximately 1 minute, whipping every 15 seconds. When the sauce thickens and is smooth, add seasonings and stir to blend.
4. Should the sauce curdle and "break", heat 1 ounce of milk to boiling. Beat the sauce, pouring in the milk slowly until it becomes smooth again.

▾ ▾ ▾   # Cheese Sauce

2 tablespoons butter
2 tablespoons flour
1 cup milk
4 ounces cream cheese
   Salt and pepper to taste
   (optional)

There are many occasions when you need a quick, versatile cream sauce for topping vegetables or other uses. Here's one I frequently use.

1. Place butter and flour in 1½-quart cook-and-measure bowl. Cook at 100% power (high), uncovered, for 1 minute, stirring as needed.
2. Add milk and cream cheese. Cook at 100% power (high), uncovered, for 2 minutes.
3. Stir to blend. Add salt and pepper, if desired, and cook at 100% power (high) uncovered, for an additional 2 minutes or until thick and smooth.

▼ ▼ ▼

Vegetable Butters

Vegetable butters are a wonderful substitute for almost anything you spread on bread or crackers. Use them for entertaining or snacking.

Onion Butter

1 large yellow onion, skinned (No need to chop, save the tears.)

Rutabega Butter

1 large begga, skinned and diced
½ cup water

Tomato Butter

4 large, ripe tomatoes, peeled, chopped and squeezed of excess water

Eggplant Butter

1 large eggplant, diced
3 ripe tomatoes or 1 can (14 oz.) stewed tomatoes

1. Place in a 1½-quart cook-and-measure bowl and cook at 100% power (high), covered, for 5 minutes. Process until smooth. Then cook at 100% power (high), uncovered, for 8 to 10 minutes or until it reaches paste consistency.

2. Place begga and water in a 1½-quart cook-and-measure bowl. Cook at 100% power (high), covered, for 10 to 12 minutes. Process until smooth. Then cook at 100% power (high), uncovered, for 8 to 10 minutes or until thick and spreadable.

3. Place in a 1½-quart cook-and-measure bowl. Cook at 100% power (high), uncovered, for 10 to 12 minutes. Process and cook at 100% power (high), uncovered, for 3 to 4 minutes, or until very thick. Add fresh grated lemon or other herbs and spices you happen to like.

   For a little extra fiber, don't peel the tomatoes.

4. Place eggplant and tomatoes in a 1½-quart cook-and-measure bowl. Cook at 100% power (high), uncovered, for 15 to 20 minutes. Stir once.

   Process and cook at 100% power (high), uncovered, for 10 minutes or until thickened. Season to taste with fresh ground pepper, lemon juice or curry powder.

Desserts

▼

Bread Pudding with
Whiskey Sauce

Low-Cal Dessert Sauce

English Apple Bake

Rummy Bananas

Prune & Peach Pie

Pear Sundae with
Almond Fudge Sauce

Your Perfect Pear

Apple Compote Cake

Delicious Apple Pie

Macadamia Nut Tulips

Plum Pudding

Upside-down
Cheesecake Ring

Coconut Pudding

▼ ▼ ▼

D E S S E R T S

▼ ▼ ▼

T he best kinds of desserts to make by
microwave are puddings, ring cakes, pies,
poached fruit, baked apples, candy and ice
cream toppings. Crusty, flaky things,
layered cakes and cookies are better suited
to cooking in a hot oven.

If you're concerned about counting
calories, make desserts with as little fat as
possible. But don't be afraid to use sugar. It
has half the calories of fat and adds so much
to taste.

One additional point about sugar.
Always use the real thing. It tastes so much
better than artificial sweeteners and it
makes things cook better. Since there are
only 16 calories per teaspoon, in a balanced
diet, there's no harm in using real sugar.

▾ ▾ ▾ Bread Pudding with Whiskey Sauce

TO SERVE 12–18

1 loaf stale bread, crushed

1 quart milk

4 eggs

2 cups sugar

2 tablespoons vanilla extract

Pinch of salt

1 cup seedless raisins

2 cans (16 oz. each) peaches, drained and sliced

¾ teaspoon nutmeg

½ teaspoon cinnamon

½ cup butter

Whiskey Sauce

1 cup brown sugar

¼ pound butter

1 egg yolk beaten with 1 tablespoon water

2 ounces whiskey

I first tasted Brad Borel's bread pudding at his restaurant in San Francisco and liked it so much I asked him to do it on the show. It converts well to microwave cooking.

1. In a large mixing bowl, mix together bread and milk. Beat eggs and add to bread and milk mixture. Beat in sugar and vanilla.

2. Mix together raisins, peaches, nutmeg, cinnamon and salt. Gently fold into the bread and milk mixture.

3. Melt butter and pour into 2-quart ring pan. Pour in pudding mixture. Cook, uncovered, at 100% power (high) for 18 to 20 minutes or until the pudding is firm.

4. Place butter and sugar in 1½-quart cook-and-measure bowl. Cook at 100% power (high) for 3 to 4 minutes, or until the sugar and butter are blended.

5. Add whiskey and stir vigorously while adding egg.

6. Pour over individual servings of pudding.

▾ ▾ ▾ Low-Cal Dessert Sauce

1 can (13 oz.) evaporated milk

½ cup sugar

3 tablespoons cornstarch, dissolved in a little evaporated milk

1 teaspoon vanilla

1 ounce liqueur of your choice or 1 teaspoon rum flavoring

Very versatile, this can be used with fruit, cake or pie. Compared to sauces made with butter and cream, this has far fewer calories.

1. Place milk, sugar, cornstarch, vanilla and liqueur in a 1½-quart cook-and-measure bowl and mix thoroughly.

2. Cook at 100% power (high) for 3 to 4 minutes or until thickened. Serve warm or cool.

English Apple Bake

TO SERVE 4

1 pound cooking apples,
cored and sliced

1 teaspoon cinnamon

¼ teaspoon cloves

1 cup granulated sugar

4 tablespoons water

½ cup mayonnaise

1 cup brown sugar

1 cup instant oatmeal

½ cup chopped hazelnuts

Nuts and apples have a special affinity that comes through regardless of the dish. Hazelnuts remind me of England, so I call this English Apple Bake.

1. Place apples, cinnamon, cloves, sugar and water in ring pan, cover and cook at 100% power (high) for 3 to 4 minutes.
2. Mix mayonnaise, brown sugar, oatmeal and hazelnuts together. Spoon over apples and press in.
3. Cook at 100% power (high), covered, for 12 to 15 minutes or until apples are tender.

Rummy Bananas

TO SERVE 6

¾ cup dark rum

½ cup dark brown sugar

2 tablespoon unsalted
butter

1 piece vanilla bean
(about 2 in.) or ½
teaspoon vanilla

2 tablespoons fresh
lemon juice

Zest of ½ lemon, cut
into strips

2 thin slices fresh ginger

6 bananas (2½ to 3
pounds)

Original recipe appears in Barbara Kafka's *Microwave Gourmet*, published by William Morrow and Company, Inc., 1987.

Barbara Kafka is one of the first conventional cookbook and food writers to recognize the microwave oven as a valuable cooking tool. Her book, "Microwave Gourmet", is creating a great deal of interest in "real" cooking by microwave. Barbara says she makes a small version of this for herself as "self-indulgence" food.

1. Combine rum, sugar, butter, vanilla bean, lemon juice, zest, and ginger in a 4-cup glass measure. (If using vanilla extract, do not add it until first cooking is completed.) Cover tightly with microwave plastic wrap. Cook at 100% power (high) for 3 minutes.
2. Remove from oven. Uncover and stir. (Add vanilla extract, if used.) Set aside.
3. Peel bananas and remove ½ inch from each end. Arrange pinwheel fashion in a 10-inch round dish. Pour rum mixture over bananas.
4. Cover tightly with plastic wrap. Cook at 100% power (high) for about 5 minutes.

▾ ▾ ▾   Prune and Peach Pie

TO SERVE 6

- 1 frozen 9-inch deep dish pie crust
- 1 package (12 oz.) pitted prunes
- 1 package (7 oz.) dried peaches
- 1 cup chopped walnuts
- ¾ cup water
- ½ cup firmly packed light brown sugar
- 4 ounces butter or margarine
- 1 teaspoon vanilla

Dried fruits are a particularly useful ingredient in microwave cooking. With a little water, they bubble up with intense flavors in a matter of minutes. Dried apricots can be substituted for peaches. Top with whipped cream if you feel a little decadent.

1. Bake pie crust according to directions on the package.
2. Put prunes, peaches, walnuts, water, sugar butter and vanilla in 1½-quart cook-and-measure bowl. Cook at 100% power (high), uncovered, for 12 minutes or until fruit moistens and expands. Stir occasionally to blend.
3. Place fruit mixture evenly in baked crust. Let cool and serve.

▾ ▾ ▾   Pear Sundae with Almond Fudge Sauce

TO SERVE 4

- 1 package (6 oz.) semi-sweet chocolate chips
- ¼ cup milk
- 2 tablespoons butter
- ½ teaspoon almond extract
- 1 quart vanilla ice cream
- 2 fresh pears, halved and cored
- Blanched sliced almonds, for garnish

Don't even consider preparing this dessert if you're watching calories. But it's terrific if you want to have something that not only looks beautiful, but tastes great as well.

1. Put chocolate, milk, butter and almond extract into 4-cup glass measuring bowl.
2. Cook at 100% power (high), uncovered, for 2 minutes, or until mixture boils. Stir once or twice while cooking. Set aside to cool.
3. Place pear halves in 1-quart casserole dish. Cover and cook at 100% power (high) for about 2 minutes, until cooked but firm.
4. Place each pear half in a dessert dish. Top with a scoop of ice cream. Pour sauce on top, then garnish with almonds.

▾ ▾ ▾   # Your Perfect Pear

TO SERVE 4

4 ripe Bosc or Barlett pears

4 tablespoons fresh orange juice or apple juice

½ teaspoon ground cinnamon

½ teaspoon freshly ground nutmeg

Recipe from DELICIOUSLY LOW: The Gourmet Guide to Low-Sodium, Low-Fat, Low-Cholesterol, Low-Sugar Cooking by Harriet Roth. Copyright 1983 by Harriet Roth. Reprinted by arrangement with NAL PEGUIN INC., New York, NY.

I love poached pears and Harriet Roth's version of this recipe is perfect in every way. Serve with raspberry sauce made from frozen raspberries, processed into a puree.

1. Core each pear from the bottom, leaving the stem intact.
2. Peel four ½-inch strips along the side of each pear.
3. Place the pears in a glass baking dish and sprinkle with the fruit juice, cinnamon and nutmeg.
4. Cover with plastic wrap and cook at 100% power (high) for 5 to 6 minutes, or until the pears are just fork tender. Be careful not to overcook.
5. Serve in individual dishes, with warm juice spooned over each pear.

▾ ▾ ▾   # Apple Compote Cake

TO SERVE 4

4 large apples, cored and sliced thinly

4 tablespoons butter

½ cup brown sugar

½ teaspoon ground cinnamon

½ teaspoon ground mace

¼ teaspoon ground nutmeg

1 ounce liqueur of choice (optional)

This flourless cake always comes out perfectly when cooked by microwave. You don't have to worry about uneven cooking.

1. Place apples in a 2-quart ring pan, lined with wax paper.
2. Combine butter, sugar, cinnamon, mace, nutmeg and liqueur in a cook-and-measure bowl and cook at 100% power (high) until the butter melts.
3. Pour mixture over apples. Cover and cook at 100% power (high) for 8 to 10 minutes or until apples are soft. Cool in refigerator for a couple of hours.
4. Press apples to bind together. Place serving platter over ring pan and invert onto platter. Remove wax paper and serve with your favorite dessert sauce.

▼ ▼ ▼   Delicious Apple Pie

TO SERVE 6

6 cooking apples,
peeled, cored and
and sliced

½ to 1 cup granulated or
firmly packed light
brown sugar

1½ tablespoon
cornstarch

¼ teaspoon ground
cinnamon

¼ teaspoon ground
nutmeg

2 frozen deep-dish pie
crusts (each 9 in.),
thawed

1 egg yolk
Salt

There are many times when microwave cooking and traditional cooking work hand-in-hand with excellent results. Apple pie is a perfect example.

1. Place apples, sugar, cornstarch, cinnamon and nutmeg in 1½-quart cook-and-measure bowl. Determine amount of sugar by sweetness of apples and your taste.
2. Cook at 100% power (high), uncovered, for 12 minutes or until apples have cooked to softness.
3. In the meantime, bake one crust following directions on the package.
4. Spread fruit into cooked pie crust. Top with second, uncooked, pie crust. Trim away excess dough and crimp around edge.
5. Place on bottom of regular oven, with heat selector set at broil, for 2 to 3 minutes or until the top crust is brown and flaky.

▼ ▼ ▼   Macadamia Nut Tulips

TO SERVE 4

¼ pound butter
½ cup sugar
½ cup light corn syrup
¼ cup flour
¼ cup crushed
macadamia nuts

Ice cream or poached
fresh fruit

The secret in making these very attractive nut shells is using buttered parchment paper. After watching Australian chef Dennis Clewes do it on my show, I tried it in the microwave oven and the fact is, it's much easier.

1. Combine butter, sugar, corn syrup, flour and macadamia nuts in a 1 1/2-quart cook-and-measure bowl. Cook at 100% power (high), uncovered, for 5 to 6 minutes, or to a taffy-like consistency.
2. Allow to cool slightly and pour 1/4 of the batter on 1-foot square of buttered parchment paper and cook at 100% power (high) for 1 1/2 to 2 minutes or until the batter starts to brown. (Note: Non-stick cooking spray can be used in

place of butter. If your oven doesn't cook evenly, turn the paper every 30 seconds or so.)

3. Again allow to cool slightly. When you can pick up the edge and it doesn't come apart, invert the paper with the shell over a 1/2-cup custard cup and peel off the paper. Press the shell onto the cup to form the tulip.

4. Let cool completely and remove from custard cup. Fill with ice cream or poached fruit.

▼ ▼ ▼   Plum Pudding

TO SERVE 8

1 cup all-purpose flour
¼ cup firmly packed light brown sugar
2 cups unseasoned bread crumbs
1 teaspoon baking soda
½ teaspoon ground nutmeg
1 teaspoon ground cinnamon
½ cup orange juice concentrate
¼ cup dark molasses
4 ounces unsalted butter or margarine
½ cup dry sherry or brandy
2 eggs
1½ cups raisins
1 ounce candied pineapple
1 ounce red and green candied cherries

One of the reasons this classic English holiday dessert is served so rarely is it takes a couple of hours to cook using traditional methods. In a microwave oven, the cooking time is 15 minutes.

1. Gradually blend together sugar, brandy and butter. Knead until fully mixed. Roll into balls about 1 inch in diameter. Place coconut on waxed paper and roll balls on coconut to cover. Chill to serve.

2. In a 1 1/2-quart cook-and-measure bowl, mix flour, brown sugar, bread crumbs, baking soda, nutmeg, cinnamon, orange juice, molasses, butter or margarine, sherry or brandy, eggs and raisins. Blend thoroughly. Press down to compact the mixture.

3. Place a covering of aluminum foil directly on the top of the mixture to prevent drying. Cover bowl with plastic wrap, unvented, to retain moisture.

4. Cook at 50% power (medium) for 15 minutes. Test for doneness by inserting skewer into center of pudding. When it comes out clean, it's done. Let stand 10 minutes.

5. To serve, place a serving platter on top of the bowl. Invert and carefully lift away the cooking bowl. Garnish with pineapple and cherries.

▼ ▼ ▼ Upside-down Cheesecake Ring

TO SERVE 6 TO 8

1 cup graham cracker
crumbs

3 tablespoons sugar

¼ cup wheat germ

3 tablespoons melted
butter

24 ounces cream cheese,
softened

3 eggs

1 cup sugar

1 cup semi-sweet
chocolate chips

1 teaspoon rum-flavored
extract

If you've seen my television programs, you know I
like to use ring pan dishes. They're perfectly suited to
microwave cooking generally and particularly to a
dish such as this cheesecake.

1. Line 2-quart ring pan with wax paper or plastic
   wrap.
2. Mix cracker crumbs, sugar, wheat germ and
   butter. Press mixture onto bottom of ring pan.
3. Blend cream cheese, eggs, sugar, chocolate chips
   and rum extract until smooth and pour over
   crust.
4. Cover with wax paper and cook at 100% power
   (high) for 12 to 15 minutes, or until set.
5. Cool. Remove wax paper. Place serving platter
   over ring pan and invert. You can spread 1 cup
   strawberry, blueberry or orange preserves on
   cream filling before inverting.

▼ ▼ ▼ Coconut Pudding

½ cup shredded
sweetened coconut

4 large eggs

1½ cups thick coconut
milk (available at
Asian food stores and
some health food
stores)

1 cup condensed milk
or whole milk

½ teaspoon ground
mace

½ teaspoon cardamom
seeds, crushed

¼ teaspoon ground
nutmeg

1 cup brown sugar

This made-from-scratch pudding is almost as easy to
make as the kind that comes in a box.

1. Cook the coconut on a plate at 100% power
   (high) for about 2 minutes, until it begins to
   brown.
2. Place eggs, coconut milk, condensed or whole
   milk, mace, cardamom, nutmeg and brown
   sugar in cook-and-measure bowl. Mix
   thoroughly and cook at 100% power (high) for
   2 to 3 minutes, whipping every 30 seconds
   until thickened.
3. Serve warm or cool, topped with browned
   coconut.

Index